Portlaoise

An Illustrated History

Portlaoise

An Illustrated History

Joe Curtis

Eastwood

First published by Eastwood Books, 2020
Dublin, Ireland
www.eastwoodbooks.com
www.wordwellbooks.com
@eastwoodbooks

First Edition

Eastwood Books is an imprint of The Wordwell Group
Eastwood Books
The Wordwell Group
Unit 9, 78 Furze Road
Sandyford
Dublin, Ireland

ISBN: 978-1-9161375-7-8

Printed in Ireland by Sprint Print..

British Library Cataloguing in Publication Data.
A catalogue record for this book is available from the British Library.

Contents

Acknowledgements

My thanks to the excellent staff of the various official sources of knowledge, including the National Library, National Archives, Irish Architectural Archive, Valuation Office, Trinity College Dublin, Representative Church Body Library (RCB), Laois County Library/Laois Local Studies, South Dublin Libraries, and in particular the following individuals: Sinead Holland (Laois Local Studies), Paul Ferguson and Paul Mulligan (Trinity College Dublin), Noel Collins (OPW), Aoife Walsh (Guinness Archives), Bernie Deasy (Delany Archive, Carlow), Damien Burke (Jesuit Archives), Redmond Photographers Roscrea, Karen Johnson (CBS Archives), Ciaran Reilly (Portlaoise Prison), Martin Cashen and Peter Doolan (Heath Golf Club), Keegan Funeral Parlour, An Garda Síochána, and Pat and Gerard McEvoy (Portlaoise Golf Club). Thanks to the various churches, schools, hospitals and businesses for showing me around their buildings, and allowing me to take photographs. Some historic information on the Prison and St Fintan's Hospital was accessed on Documenting Ireland: Parliament, People and Migration (www.dippam.ac.uk).

All sources of photos are acknowledged individually, unless taken from the author's own collection.

Introduction

The English stronghold in Ireland in the sixteenth century centred on the Dublin region, called 'The Pale', but they were continually trying to penetrate further into the territories of Irish chieftains. In the midlands, around the year 1548, the English built a fort in the Laoghaise (or Leix) region to guard against attacks by the O'Moores and O'Connors, and this was known as Fort Protector (after Lord Somerset, the Lord Protector of the Crown). In 1556, Queen Mary I decided on the 'plantation' of the Irish territories by confiscating their land and giving it to English 'settlers', calling the area Queen's County and stipulating that Fort Leix (Port Laoghaise) be renamed Mary Burgh. In 1570, her successor, Queen Elizabeth I, granted a charter officially making the town into a borough, a status it held until 1830.

The fort was roughly square in shape, encompassing about 2 acres, and various houses and other buildings sprang up around the outside, including St Peter's church on the west side, which is reputed to have been built in 1560. Fighting between the new English settlers and the native Irish resulted in the town being badly damaged a few times, and it was reported that in 1598, the fort housed up to 200 soldiers and a few horsemen. After the Cromwellian campaign in 1650, the fort was abandoned and partly demolished by the Parliamentarians under Hewson.

However, in the eighteenth century, the town outside of the actual fort walls continued to develop, and a long main street and market square set the general pattern for its layout. Some of the buildings were probably single storey and built of mud, to be rebuilt later in stone to a greater height.

Aerial photo of Portlaoise in the 1950s. (*Courtesy of National Library of Ireland.*)

Redevelopment of the town continued into the next century; the new St Peter's church (Anglican) was built further to the west in 1803/04, and various public buildings and institutions followed over the next few decades.

However, the town layout was dictated by the fort walls, with Main Street on the south side, Railway Street on the west, Tower Hill on the north, and Church Avenue to the east. Today, there are numerous remnants of the old fort walls to be seen in these streets, while other stone masonry is incorporated into new buildings or new boundary walls. The curved north-east 'bastion' of the original fort is still standing, and is not as powerful as it looks, since the inside is hollow, and the stonework is not thick.

There was a sixteenth-century 'Stone House' on the east side of the fort, which later became the county infirmary, and its circular tower was incorporated into the Presentation Convent when the nuns purchased and redeveloped the property in 1824. Presumably this is not a spelling mistake, instead of 'Store House', meaning a shop of some sort, as a store could be expected to have been located inside the fort for protection. Assuming that the word 'Stone' is correct, would this imply that other buildings in the town were inferior, built of mud or timber?

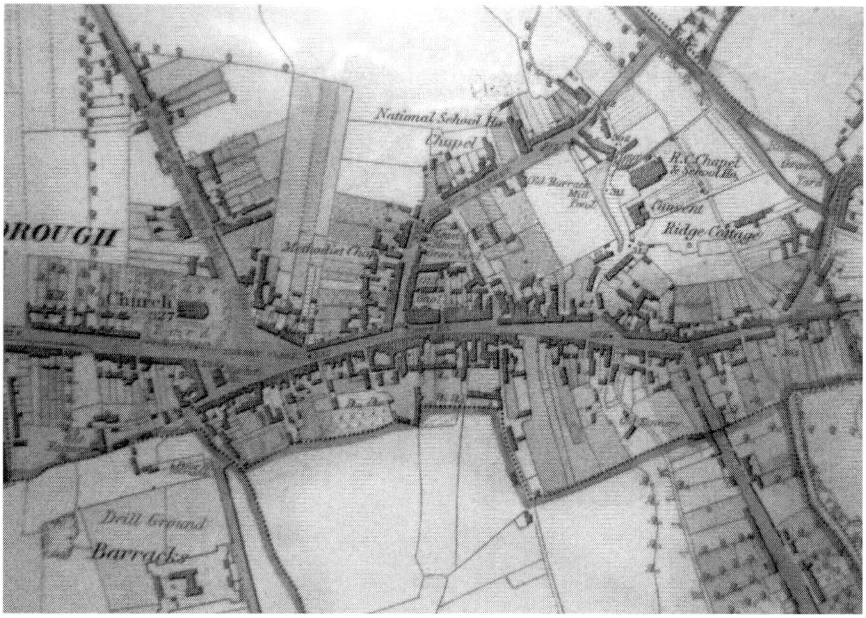

Ordnance Survey map of Maryborough, 1839. (*Courtesy of Trinity College Dublin.*)

Ordnance Survey map of Maryborough, 1889. (*Courtesy of Trinity College Dublin.*)

The town was renamed Portlaoise in the 1920s, meaning 'Fort of Laoghaise', but people who were born in that era continued to use the name Maryborough (pronounced 'Mar Bra' by locals) throughout their lives, doing so right up to the present day.

Nowadays the town is effectively in two halves, with the modern, bland shopping centre and council offices on the south side, accessed from the 1970 James Fintan Lawlor Avenue (ring road), while the Main Street is the centre of the old quarter, mostly the entertainment district. The latter district would benefit from a focal point, such as a big mill pond in the centre of the former fort. Ideally it would have a replica stone mill on an island, accommodating craft workshops and a civic museum, all commemorating the Odlums Mill, which was a big enterprise just outside the east wall of the former fort for nearly 150 years, complete with its mill race and mill pond, fed from the River Triogue.

The coming of the motorway in 1997, while bypassing the town, in fact makes the town more accessible and appealing, and on the north side, the railway has never been busier. Traffic in the town is free flowing because of the clever use of numerous zebra crossings for pedestrians.

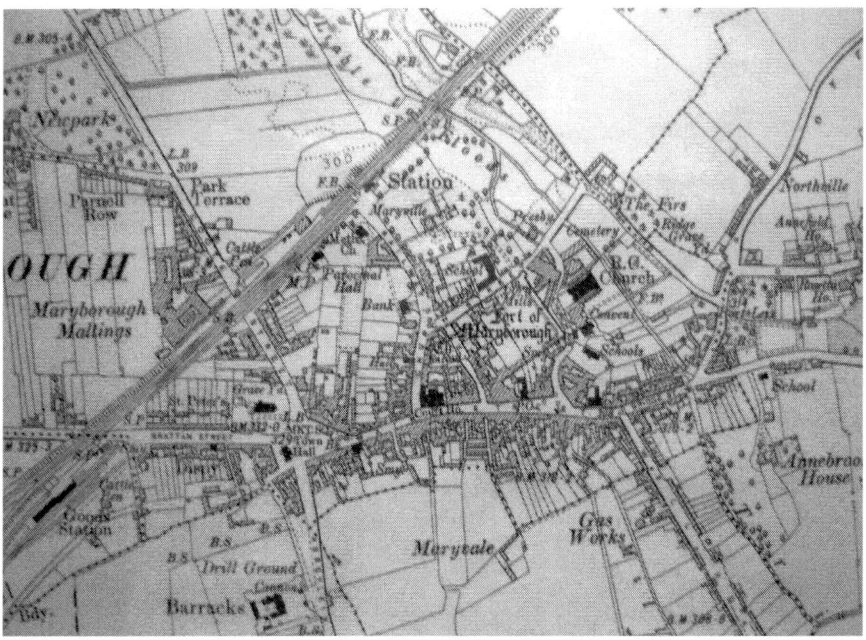

Ordnance Survey map of Maryborough, 1907. (*Courtesy of Trinity College Dublin.*)

ONE

Religion

St Peter's (Anglican), Grattan Street

The first Anglican church was built on Church Street in 1560, during the reign of the English monarch Elizabeth I, the last of the Tudor line. The present St Peter's was built some distance away, at the corner of Market Square, in 1804, with the address given as Quality Row in Griffith's Valuation in the 1850s.

The tower, with its obelisk-shaped spire, was designed by the famous English architect James Gandon, who also designed the neoclassical Custom House in Dublin. Internally, there are galleries to the sides and rear, the latter accommodating the pipe organ by Bevington of London (the Odlum family paid for an electric bellows in 1958, replacing the original hand-operated bellows). Besides the usual collection of memorial tablets, there is one to Dr David Jacob, who died in 1912. There is only one small stained-glass panel in the centre-north of the nave, entitled 'Christ Blessing Children' (1938), by the famous Alfred Ernest Child of An Túr Gloine (Tower of Glass) Studio in Dublin.

The hollow square tower (it has no internal floors) of the original church is still standing in the corner of the old graveyard, accessed now from Railway Street. One wonders if the bell was transferred to the new church in 1804. Thankfully, the baptismal and burial records, dating from 1793, were successfully transferred to the new church.

The rectory was in various locations over the years, including Portran House on the Stradbally Road and 25 Coote Street (immediately north of the Maltings).

The Anglican parochial hall on Station Road was built in 1883 by Tom Turpin, and donated by him to the congregation that same year. Tom Turpin once owned the site where Mince Norton had a malting works. Nowadays, the hall is still owned by St Peter's, but is leased out on Sundays to a Pentecostal church with mostly Congolese members, who rejoice in good lively music and singing.

The church of St John the Baptist at Ballyfin is administered by this parish, and likewise the small Holy Trinity church (1843) beside the Rock of Dunamase.

Methodist church, Railway Street

John Wesley, the founder of the English Methodist Church, is reputed to have preached in 1775 in a shed in Bull Lane, which was the first venue for their place of worship in Portlaoise.

By 1798, they had built a proper chapel in Church Street (only the Anglican/Established Church could use the term 'church' to describe their place of worship, until Disestablishment in 1869).

The foundation stone for the present church opposite the railway station was laid on 9 May 1883, and a silver trowel was presented to Mrs Hipwell, after which, lunch was served to guests in the grand jury room (local government) above the courthouse. Mr Sidwell of Dublin built the Gothic-style church in seven months, at a total cost of £1,470, including architect's fees, and it could hold 160 people. The foundation stone for 'Wesleyan Chapel AD 1798' is now embedded in the boundary wall of the present church.

For a while, the old Methodist church building at the corner of Church Street and Jessop Street was used as a parochial hall, but it later fell into commercial use and is now occupied by a firm of architects. In 2001, the Methodists built a small parochial hall to the south of their present church.

St Peter & Paul's Catholic church, Dublin Road

Portlaoise was a plantation town, full of English Protestant settlers brought over during the plantation of Laois and Offaly in the sixteenth century. Gradually, the native Irish Catholics regained a foothold in the area, and Catholic priests are recorded in Maryborough (Portlaoise) from at least 1656, when

Fr Paul Cashin was parish priest. He was succeeded by Fr Malone, Fr Lawlor, Fr Barron, Fr O'Neill, and then Fr Nicholas O'Connor in the opening years of the nineteenth century. Judging from the 1839 Ordnance Survey map, the Catholics had a chapel and also a schoolhouse on the site of the present Christian Brothers School (CBS) on Tower Hill. Some say that the Catholics used the old St Peter's church after the Anglicans moved to their new church in 1804, but that is highly unlikely.

Very Revd Nicholas O'Connor, parish priest for forty years from at least 1815 (he died in 1855, aged 75), was responsible for building the new chapel in present-day Church Avenue. In 1822, the foundation stone for the rectangular chapel of St Peter & Paul (to distinguish it from the Anglican church of St Peter) was laid. A very basic chapel was in operation from around 1823, but was not officially consecrated until 1826. Initially, the people had to stand during the Mass, but in due course, seating was installed. In the 1860s, during the tenure of parish priest Dr Taylor, the chancel and three galleries were built, in addition to the installation of an organ and a church bell. The ashlar-stone west façade and towers were added in 1872.

During Dr Murphy's time (1901-40), refinements were made, including a pulpit, parquet flooring in the central and side aisles, central heating, Stations of the Cross, marble altar rails, baptistry mosaics, mosaics of The Last Supper in the sanctuary, and new statues. The ribbed and vaulted plastered ceilings were probably an embellishment after the church was built. However, partly due to the lack of car parking, and the overbearing presence of Odlums Flour Mill right beside it, the church did not stand the test of time, and closed in 1965. Surprisingly, nobody could find an alternative use for this fine building, and so it was demolished in the 1980s. Various parish priests were buried inside the old church, and their remains were moved to the grounds of the new church in 1965.

A new church had been planned from around 1940, during the Second World War ('The Emergency' in neutral Ireland), and the enormous sum of £200,000 was collected by parishioners by running dances, garden fêtes, sales of work, whist drives, bingo, and the like. The foundation stone was laid in September 1963, and by July 1965 the church was ready for formal consecration by Monsignor Brennan, the parish priest of Edenderry. This was a huge social event in the town, attended by the great and the good, and afterwards, the Presentation nuns laid on a meal in the convent for the dignitaries whilst parishioners partook of refreshments in the St Mary's CBS Hall.

The new red-bricked church, with its tall free-standing bell tower, was positioned in a very prominent and busy location, facing down Bridge Street. It was built by J.J. Jennings of Dún Laoghaire, County Dublin, to a design by Jones & Kelly of Dublin. The new church incorporated some items from the previous one, such as the Stations of the Cross, the 'plate' (gold chalice, etc.), the marble side altar, and the baptismal font. A new organ was installed in October 1966. Initially the altar was against the back wall, and the priest would recite the Mass in Latin, with his back to the congregation, but gradually, after the Second Vatican Council in the mid-1960s, English was adopted, and the priest faced his parishioners.

The presbytery was at the north end of Church Avenue, then, in 1912, the priests bought Portleix House, opposite the present church (which had originally been built in 1810 for the famous Dr John Jacob), and they renamed it St Joseph's. Extra priests were sometimes accommodated in Maryville behind the CBS, on land once called Golden Croft, but the house is now boarded up.

The spacious parish centre beside the church was opened in 2005.

The homely church of the Assumption on the Heath is administered by St Peter & Paul's parish, and dates from 1836. The freestanding bell frame contains a bell cast in 1930 by Mathew O'Byrne of Dublin, which was donated by John Fitzpatrick of Dunamase. The ruin of the older Killenny church is in the field behind.

The third church in this parish is the cruciform church of the Holy Cross at Ratheniska, which dates from the early nineteenth century.

Other Churches

Griffith's Valuation of 1850 lists the Zion Independent Chapel at 23 Church Lane, beside the recent CBS (which was probably the main Catholic chapel prior to 1826). This was then under Revd Hugh Torrens.

The Religious Society of Friends (Quakers) had many Laois connections, such as the Pims from Mountmellick. There was a Quaker Meeting House (church) in Bridge Street, Mountrath, in the nineteenth century, and even today the town has a Quaker burial ground and public park at the east end of Main Street. The plot contains the remains of 590 people, interred from 1691-1919, but the actual headstones were moved to their Rosenalis cemetery.

St Peter's church (Anglican), built in 1804, enhances the west end of Portlaoise.

Above left: The interior of St Peter's church is interesting.

Above right: The three galleries of St Peter's, with impressive pipe organ.

Above left: St Peter's vestry, under the tower, with photos of various clerics.

Above right: The 1883 Parochial Hall of St Peter's on Station Road is leased to an African church.

Below: The tower (built 1560) of the original St Peter's is still standing on Railway Street. The attractive 'street art' or mural on the adjacent wall is the work of Dunamase College students, which now occupies the former technical school opposite the graveyard.

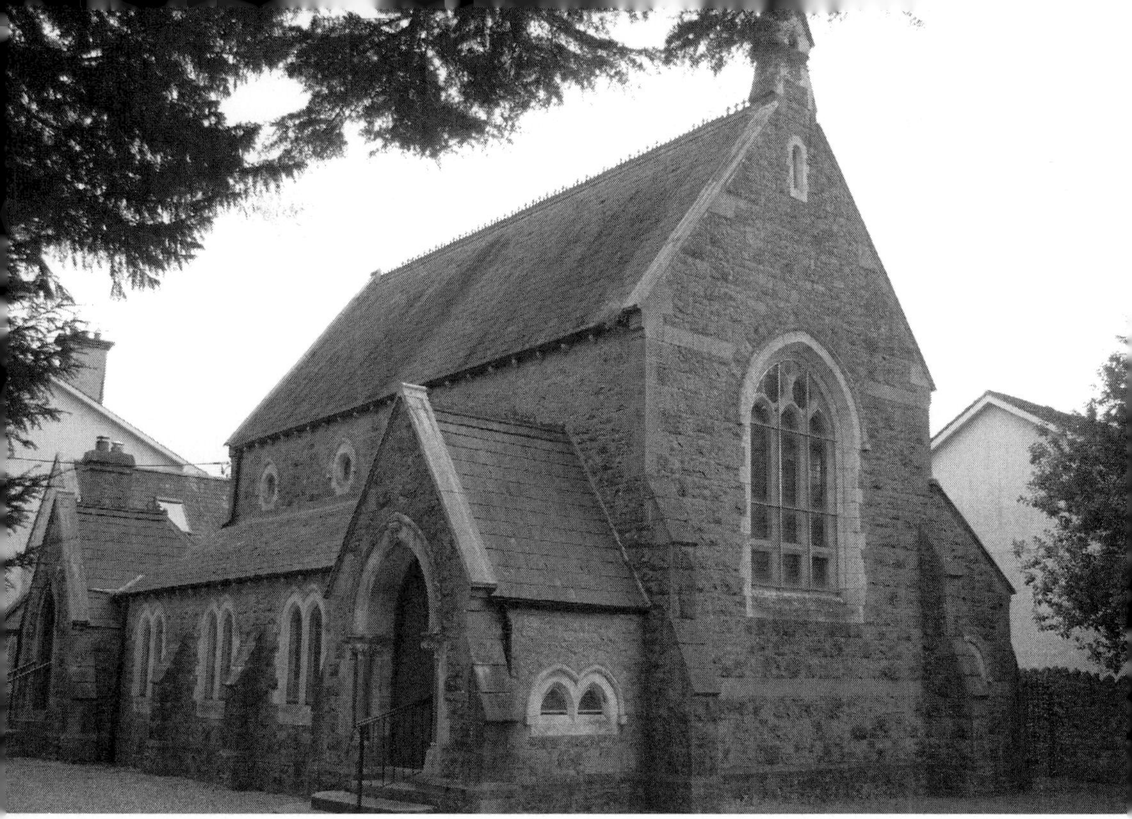

Methodist church (built 1883), opposite the railway station, which is still in use.

The interior of the Methodist church is plain and simple.

The former Methodist church (built 1798) on Church Street is now an architect's office.

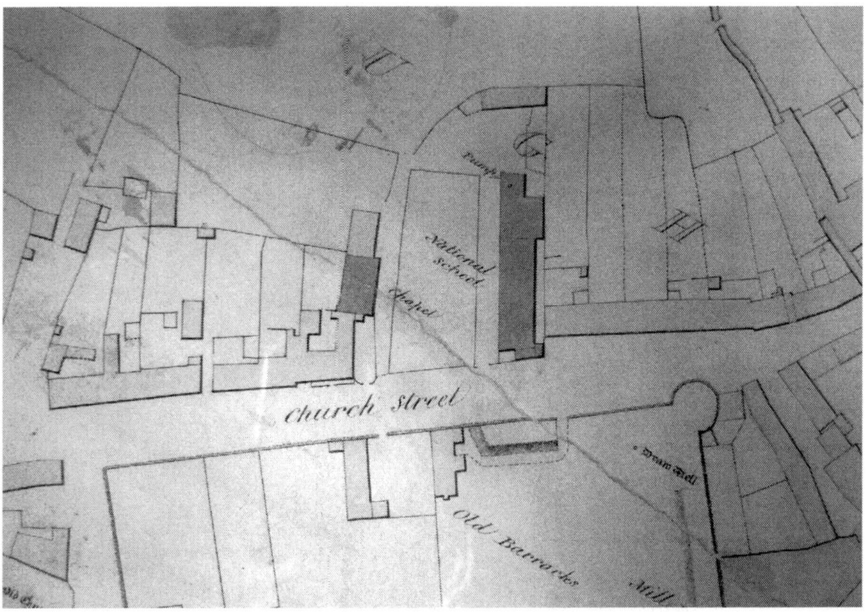

Ordnance Survey map (1839) of the site where the Christian Brothers settled in 1847, showing an existing school and a chapel opposite. This was probably the original Catholic chapel, which then became the Zion chapel in 1846. (*Courtesy of National Archives.*)

Early twentieth-century front and rear views of the church of St Peter & Paul, and the Presentation Convent. Note the Mill Pond and Head Race on Church Avenue. (*Courtesy of National Library of Ireland.*)

Above left: Vandalised interior of the church of St Peter & Paul before demolition in the 1980s. (*Courtesy of* Glimpses of Portlaoise *by John O'Brien & Teddy Fennelly.*)

Above right: Rear of the church of St Peter & Paul. The basement under the big window was the schoolhouse, built in 1822, and taken over by the Presentation Sisters in 1824 at the invitation of the parish priest Revd N. O'Connor. (*Courtesy of CBS Archives.*)

Church of St Peter & Paul, built in 1965.

Church of St Peter & Paul, as seen from the overgrown Ridge Graveyard, with St Joseph's Presbytery on right (now empty).

Above left: The interior of the church of St Peter & Paul is plain and simple.

Above right: This baptismal font provides a link with the lovely old St Peter & Paul church.

Above: Group of priests (1980). Left to right: Fr Don Shelly, Fr Barry O'Connell, Fr Billy Mathews, Fr Mathews, Fr Matt Walsh, Fr T. Browne, Fr Pat Collier, Fr Paul Maher, Fr Denis Delaney. (*Courtesy of Redmonds Photography, Roscrea.*)

Left: Fr Nicholas O'Connor, parish priest of the church of St Peter & Paul (1815-1855), who brought the Presentation nuns and the Christian Brothers to Portlaoise. (*Courtesy of CBS Archives.*)

Group of altar boys in St Peter & Paul, 1958. (*Courtesy of CBS Archives.*)

Junior choir of St Peter & Paul, with Christian Brother in centre, 1947. (*Courtesy of CBS Archives.*)

Church of the Assumption, the Heath, built in 1836 by Fr N. O'Connor.

The fifteenth-century ruins of St Fintan's church in Clonenagh cemetery, between Portlaoise and Mountrath.

TWO

Education

The 1835 Second Report of the Commission on Education recorded ten schools in Portlaoise (Maryborough), the two main ones being a national school kept by Mr Gibson (presumably Catholic), with 253 boys on the roll, and a convent national school, with 221 girls on the roll. The boys' school received £15 per annum from the National Board of Education, while the girls' school received £10, and both schools also received small payments from the children. Actual daily attendance was usually far lower than the numbers on the rolls.

It seems that the Protestant children attended Ellen Boyle's school (seventy-four girls), sponsored by the London Hibernian Society, or Mr T. Boyle's school (seventy boys), sponsored by the Society for Discountenancing Vice.

There were also four very small private schools and two hedge schools, one run by Jane Finlay for six boys and four girls, and the other run by Patrick Scurlock for twenty-six boys and twelve girls. These hedge schools were usually held in a cottage or outbuilding of basic quality.

St Mary's Christian Brothers School, Tower Hill

The CBS site was the centre of Catholic worship and education long before the Christian Bothers arrived. The Ordnance Survey Town Plan of 1839 shows a national school, and a chapel to the west of the site. The Valuation Office House Books of 1843 record Fr Nicholas O'Connor, parish priest, living in the two-storey house here and renting out a school room, 46ft by 24ft by 11ft high.

The Brothers, led by Br James Vincent Culkin, arrived in 1847, taking over the existing basic lay school, and then built a new school-cum-monastery fronting the public road within a year or two. A few years later, Fr O'Connor moved into Golden Croft (later named Maryville), leaving his old house to the Brothers. In 1886, the Brothers applied to the Board of Education for a grant, stating that the existing school was timber framed, with a galvanised iron roof, size 50ft by 25ft by 11ft high, but it wasn't until 1906 that an extension was added as a west wing of their 1840s building. Thereafter, the ground floor of the entire school was the primary school, and the first floor was the secondary school.

The 1901 Census records five Brothers, aged 18, 21, 22, 29 and 32. The 1911 Census records a change in political mood, since it was defiantly completed in old Irish by all five Brothers, with a note added by a third party: 'Monks All'. In the 1890s, the Brothers had built a new rear monastery, including a first-floor chapel.

Christian Brothers Schools were famous throughout Ireland for teaching boys the accordion, and in Portlaoise they went further, and had their own marching band for public occasions. Besides Gaelic football, the Brothers also played handball (the open-air concrete ball alley is still there), which only required a hand to smack the ball, long before squash rackets brought the sport indoors.

The Christian Brothers built a new primary school on Borris Road, called St Paul's, which opened in 1964, leaving the entire Tower Hill premises as their secondary school. The Brothers vacated their original monastery in 1984 and moved into Maryville behind (which was previously occupied by the parish priest), and they built playing pitches around it.

In 2010, St Mary's CBS secondary school moved to a separate new building on the same marvellous campus as the Presentation girls' Scoil Chríost Rí, about a mile from town on the Borris Road, the nearest thing the two religious communities call co-educational.

In 2017, St Paul's CBS primary school amalgamated with the Presentation nuns' two schools, Sacred Heart and Scoil Mhuire, on a new primary-school campus at Aughnaharna on the Stradbally Road, named Holy Family Schools.

Currently, Maryville monastery on Station Road is boarded up, and St Paul's on Borris Road is being rebuilt as St Francis Special School. The original CBS school on Tower Hill is now used by the Education & Training Board (ETB) as Portlaoise Further Education Centre, providing various courses for adults.

Presentation Convent School, Church Avenue

The Presentation nuns were invited to Portlaoise from Carlow in 1824, two years after the adjoining church of St Peter & Paul was built, for the purpose of running the Catholic girls' school. The girls' school was incorporated into the rear basement of the church, under the altar, and it comprised two classrooms, each 20ft by 17ft.

They took up residence in the adjacent old infirmary, which was a two-storey building in poor condition. (It had been constructed around a sixteenth-century 'Stone House' to the east of the original fort.) The nuns immediately added a chapel on the north-east side of the building, and probably the other two rear extensions. However, the conversion of the old infirmary was ultimately unsuccessful; the old front part of the convent was demolished in 1872, and the present very tall three-storey convent built. Thankfully, the 28ft-high circular tower from the ancient 'Stone House' was retained and extended in height.

The nuns moved out of the basement school at the rear of St Peter & Paul's church around 1843, after building a two-storey five-room school abutting the south-west side of the convent (45ft by 27ft by 20ft high, with a 21ft by 16ft by 20ft return). One room was later designated the industrial school, where embroidery, sewing and knitting were taught. In 1888, a new national school was built some distance to the south of the convent, being two storey and detached, with four rooms (each 30ft by 20ft by 14ft), after receiving a grant of £512 towards the £768 cost.

Samuel Lewis, writing in 1837, records a superioress and sixteen nuns in the convent. By the time of the 1901 Census, there were twenty-three nuns and two servants, and this number had increased to thirty by the time of the 1911 Census.

In 1931, the Sacred Heart National School (*Scoil an Clochair*, Irish for 'Convent School', is inscribed in the plasterwork) was built abutting Church Avenue, as an extension of the 1888 building.

Scoil Mhuire was the next of the building projects, in 1955, but this national school was built across the road from the convent, inside the former fort site.

Secondary education was never to the forefront of the nuns' endeavours, although they probably operated a 'secondary top', allowing girls to stay in the national school to do their Intermediate (Junior) Certificate. This was formalised in 1968, the year after free secondary education was introduced by the government, when Scoil Chríost Rí (Christ the King) was built to the very south of the schoolyard. The three-storey secondary school was almost identical to the new St Paul's CBS on Borris Road. In 2010, the girls moved to the new Scoil Chríost Rí secondary school on Borris Road, on the same campus as the new CBS secondary school, where they share sports facilities, and for some unknown reason the older secondary school on Church Avenue was demolished soon afterwards.

The year 2017 was a sad one for the town of Portlaoise, when the nuns' two primary schools moved, with the CBS primary school, to the fabulous Holy Family schools campus on Stradbally Road. Scoil Mhuire is now used part-time as a music school run by the council, but the convent and old school buildings lie empty. In 2008, deceased nuns' remains were exhumed from their private cemetery behind the convent, and moved to a new plot in St Peter & Paul's cemetery.

Scoil Bhríde National School, Harpur Lane

This mixed Catholic school only opened in 1986 but quickly expanded, requiring eleven prefabs to be installed. They recently moved to a lovely new building on the opposite side of the road, to the north of Portlaoise College.

Maryborough National School, Educate Together, Gaelscoil, Stradbally Road

The Church of Ireland (Anglican) national school, supported by the Church Education Society, was a two-roomed building opposite the present church of St Peter & Paul as far back as at least the 1820s (it is shown on an 1823 map). It was rebuilt in 1828, and again in 1895, with a grant of £220 towards the latter's £330 cost, and extended to the rear in subsequent years.

In 2014, the national school moved to Summerhill, off the Stradbally Road (near Holy Family schools), on the same wonderful and spacious campus as a new Gaelscoil (founded in 1998), and a new Educate Together (founded in 2010), both national schools.

Portlaoise College, Mountrath Road

This fine mixed and non-denominational second-level school was built on a green-field site in 2006, as a replacement for the technical school on Railway Street/Tower Hill.

Maryborough Technical School has been the backbone of practical education in Portlaoise since 1907, when the first school was built, providing skills for the various businesses and manufacturers in the town. Renamed

Portlaoise Vocational School in 1930, the school was extended to the south in 1937, and remodelled and further extended south in 1963. The old school now houses Dunamase College, a secondary school run by the Education and Training Board.

Portlaoise Institute, a third-level college, is on the same campus as Portlaoise College, and provides a variety of practical diploma courses, in addition to post-Leaving Certificate courses.

Brigidine Convent Boarding School, Coote Street, Mountrath

Many of the prosperous farmers around Portlaoise sent their daughters to the Brigidine Convent boarding school in Mountrath, which also accepted day pupils. The Convent of St Brigid was founded by Bishop Delany in Tullow, County Carlow, in 1807, and another convent was built in Mountrath in 1809. This was extended in 1837 to provide for boarders, and again in 1886 with St Joseph's wing. In 2009, the nuns amalgamated with the Patrician Brothers of Ballyfin College, and St Aengus Vocational School (founded 1969), in the new community secondary school in front of the town cemetery.

Patrician College Boarding School, Ballyfin, near Mountrath

The wealthy farmers around the Portlaoise area sent their sons to the exclusive Patrician Brothers secondary boarding in Ballyfin near Mountrath. The beautiful classical building was built on an existing house site by local landlord Sir Charles Coote in the 1820s, to a design by Richard and William Morrison. Besides the beautiful internal plasterwork (stucco), other special features included the mid-nineteenth-century Richard Turner conservatory (orangery) at the rear of the house, and the 28-acre man-made lake. The walled demesne, including the two walled gardens, was laid out by other members of the Coote family at least a century before the present house was built.

The demesne had its own private chapel for the owners and staff, built in the 1790s but extended later. After Disestablishment in 1869, the church was open to the Anglican public, and St John the Baptist church is nowadays part of St Peter's Parish in Portlaoise (and also The Rock in Dysart Enos under the Rock of Dunamase).

From 1930 to 2009, the house was known as Ballyfin College, a boys' secondary boarding school run by the Patrician Brothers. The Brothers also ran it as a big working farm, with extensive farm buildings near the school. The Brothers amalgamated with the Brigidine nuns in Mountrath in 2009 in the new community school.

The monastery of St Patrick was founded by Bishop Delany in Tullow in 1808 (one year after the Brigidine nuns' convent was established), and it spread to Mountrath in 1810. Their boarding school and monastery fronted onto Coote Street on the same campus as the Brigidine nuns, but later was expanded to the north side of Coote Street, roughly opposite the nuns. In 1886, there were 100 pupils in the boarding school, plus 13 Brothers and 28 novices in the monastery.

The Brothers' original school buildings are still standing in Mountrath, but in new usage, and the Brigidine Convent buildings are partly in alternative use. The rear Brigidine cemetery contains the graves of deceased nuns, and also some Patrician Brothers (including one from 1822), but most of the Brothers' remains were removed from Ballyfin College and reinterred in Ballyfin parish graveyard. The Brothers and Sisters still run primary schools in Mountrath: St Fintan's (built 1976) and Scoil Bhríde (built in 1984).

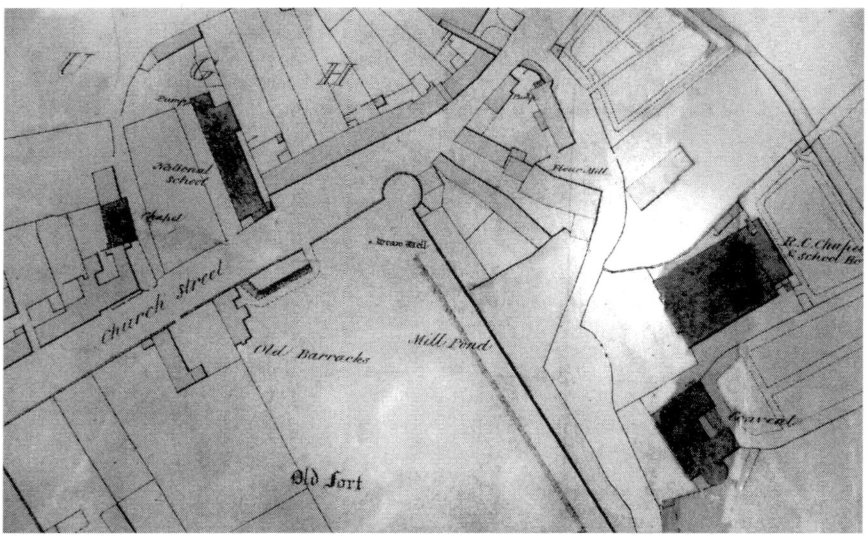

Ordnance Survey map (1839) with site of future CBS school on left, and Presentation nuns' school at rear of church. The convent was the former 'Stone House', then infirmary, and was rebuilt in 1872. (*Courtesy of Trinity College Dublin.*)

View of Christian Brothers School, 1947. (*Courtesy of CBS Archives.*)

Current view of CBS school, with monastery to the rear. The latter building was originally the priests' house before the Brothers arrived in 1847.

Above: Rear view of CBS school and monastery, including the 1905 extension. Note the remains of the tall handball alley on right.

Left: CBS monastery, with first-floor chapel on left. The iconic arched doorway was the setting for many school photos. (*Courtesy of CBS Archives.*)

Ballyfin Demesne, the house and its estate of 614 acres, was bought by an American couple, and since 2011 they have operated it as a very exclusive five-star hotel, with only twenty bedrooms. The Brothers' three-storey block to the right of the house has been replaced by a small two-storey building. The 120ft round tower behind the hotel was built as a folly during the Famine era of the 1840s, complete with moat and drawbridge, to provide work (and money) for the locals. Today, it can again be accessed by hotel guests via an internal spiral staircase.

Above: The now boarded-up Maryville, behind the CBS school, was a two-storey residence for priests and brothers.

Below: CBS scholarship group, 1929-1935. (*Courtesy of CBS Archives.*)

CBS centenary celebrations (1947), with pupil Donal Gannon welcoming Bishop Keogh and Brother Ennis – the priest has the thicker of the white 'dog collars'. (*Courtesy of CBS Archives.*)

Teaching staff in the CBS, including a few laymen, 1947. (*Courtesy of CBS Archives.*)

First class in the CBS school, 1947. (*Courtesy of CBS Archives.*)

Combined Intermediate (now called Junior) and Leaving Certificate group, CBS school, 1947/48. (*Courtesy of CBS Archives.*)

The Portlaoise CBS entry for Leinster Colleges' Junior Hurling Team, 1947/48, with Christian Brother in centre. (*Courtesy of CBS Archives.*)

CBS Portlaoise achieved first place in Feis Laoise in 1947. Team pictured with Christian Brother in centre. (*Courtesy of CBS Archives.*)

CBS Portlaoise hurling team, 1953. (*Courtesy of CBS Archives.*)

CBS Leaving Certificate class of 1952/53. (*Courtesy of CBS Archives.*)

CBS school choir pictured in the mid-1950s, featuring trophies, long trousers, short pants and assorted ties. (*Courtesy of CBS Archives.*)

Portlaoise Cadets in the Knights of Malta (1962), including CBS lads. (*Courtesy of CBS Archives.*)

CBS Leaving Certificate class of 1963 in the school yard with statue behind. (*Courtesy of CBS Archives.*)

CBS school band of 1963/64 in the school yard, featuring tin whistles, button accordions and drums. (*Courtesy of CBS Archives.*)

CBS Portlaoise were Leinster champions in 1987/88. (*Courtesy of CBS Archives.*)

St Paul's CBS, Borris Road, 6th class, 1994/95. (*Courtesy of CBS Archives.*)

St Paul's CBS, Borris Road, Sports Day, 1995. This modern building is now gone, and St Francis Special School is currently being built on the site. (*Courtesy of CBS Archives.*)

Presentation Convent (1872) on left, two-storey national school (1843) in middle, and Sacred Heart Convent School (1931) on right (this was an extension to the 1888 school hidden behind it).

Scoil Mhuire National School was built by the nuns in 1955, across the road from the convent, and is now used by the council for music classes.

South elevation of the empty Presentation Convent, with circular tower (extended in height in 1872) from the sixteenth-century 'Stone House'.

Group of students in Presentation school, 1967. (*Courtesy of Redmonds Photography, Roscrea.*)

Beautifully attired convent girls pictured with nun in the centre. (*Courtesy of Redmonds Photography, Roscrea.*)

Convent in the vanguard. (*Courtesy of Redmonds Photography, Roscrea.*)

No longer convent girls. (*Courtesy of Redmonds Photography, Roscrea.*)

Beautifully composed picture of Presentation nuns on the steps at the rear of their convent. (*Courtesy of Redmonds Photography, Roscrea.*)

Brigidine Convent and boarding school in Mountrath.

Official closing of the Brigidine Convent schools in Mountrath, 2009.

Brigidine student releases a dove during the ceremony to mark the closing of the convent school in Mountrath, 2009.

The former technical school in Portlaoise is now Dunamase College, a secondary school.

Mosaic logo on the floor in the 1963 wing of Dunamase College. '*Scientia Potentia Est*' is Latin for 'Knowledge is Power'.

Maryborough Anglican National School. (*Courtesy of Redmonds Photography, Roscrea.*)

Patrician College, Ballyfin, 1983. (*Courtesy of Lar Cooke.*)

Josephine Curtis (*née* Haslam) from Gorteen/Cappagh reminisces in 1984 about school plays presented by the Patrician College and the Brigidine Convent, Mountrath, in the 1920s and '30s.

Present-day Coote Street, looking towards the centre of Mountrath. The gabled terraces on both sides of the road were originally the Patrician monastery and schools.

The Rory O'Connor School of Dancing in Portlaoise in the 1970s. (*Courtesy of Redmonds Photography, Roscrea.*)

THREE

Health

St Fintan's Hospital, Dublin Road

Mental illness was not really understood in the past, and the term 'lunatic' was applied to anyone not strictly conforming to the norm – even elderly patients with mild dementia. The government's solution was to lock up everyone who could not be understood or cured with conventional medicine. Hence, lunatic asylums were built all over the country, mostly of similar design and construction, utilising austere grey ashlar limestone.

Maryborough District Lunatic Asylum, which catered for a few midland counties, opened on 14 May 1833, with the central block used as the governor's residence, offices, etc. Matching extensions were built to the north and south during 1863–66. Two new wings in red brick followed in 1898, and two more again in 1936–37. A fever hospital was built to the rear around 1900.

The Government Inspector's Report for 1835 recorded sixty-four males and fifty-nine females, although the building was designed for one hundred patients. Ten patients died in the first fifteen months after the asylum opened. The men worked on the 14 acres, laying out paths, building walls and ditches, and tending to potatoes and vegetables. The women were engaged in spinning, knitting, needlework and laundry. The asylum made a profit from the sale of the patients' produce. Dr John Jacob was the medical consultant to the asylum.

The Government Report for 1844 provides further information about the asylum, including recording the appointment of two chaplains, at £30 per annum each. There were eighty single cells, twelve four-bed cells, two large dormitories with eighteen beds in each, ten day rooms, and two workrooms.

Diet consisted of oatmeal and potatoes, grown on the farm, and beef soup on three days a week. Bread and milk was served for supper. The pigs ate any leftovers and were later killed for food.

The gaol across the road also held lunatics, presumably those thought to be too dangerous to be housed in the asylum.

In 1925, the asylum changed its name to Portlaoise District Mental Hospital, and in 1983 it was changed to St Fintan's Psychiatric Hospital.

From the 1830s, farming and outdoor work appealed to the rural patients in the hospital, and in fact was regarded by the doctors as part of their treatment. Therefore, additional land was purchased for farming activities, including outlying farms such as at Shaen near Emo. As recently as 1983, the hospital farmed about 252 acres, handling sheep, cattle and pigs, and growing vegetables.

Although the hospital was initially self-contained and self-sufficient, in the second half of the twentieth century, it began to invite the public to such events as annual dances, which proved very popular with Portlaoise residents.

Nowadays, the hospital is an open campus; there are only a few resident patients, but various mental health facilities and advisors are available to the general public. Alvernia House was opened in 2016 for the Irish Wheelchair Association in the old red-brick wing on the east side of the hospital.

The hospital catered for the patients' religious needs, initially using space inside the building as a shared chapel. In the mid-1890s, a unique twin building was erected to the west of the campus, comprising a small Protestant church and a big Catholic chapel, linked by a double entrance and a shared mortuary. The Protestant space is very small and plain, whereas the larger Catholic space is enhanced by the three-light sanctuary window, with three marvellous Harry Clarke stained-glass windows.

Naturally, a very large number of patients died here since 1833, bearing in mind that many patients were in old age when admitted. Even though most of these Christians were baptised as infants, confirmed as children, and even married as young adults, it seems that most were not afforded a Christian burial to assist them on their way to Heaven. There is a tiny cemetery to the south-west of the hospital, more in the nature of a mass grave, but it wasn't until 2008 that a small headstone was erected to commemorate the many unnamed patients who were buried here from 1833 to 1898. After the St Peter & Paul's cemetery opened in 1897, a plot was opened for future unnamed patients of St Fintan's.

You might wonder why the hospital was renamed as St Fintan's in 1983. A few miles south of Portlaoise there is a small townland called Clonenagh, which contains the fifteenth-century ruins of St Fintan's monastic church, which sits in the middle of an old cemetery. St Fintan is reputed to have founded the monastery here in the year 548. Across the road is an extension of the cemetery, and outside the entrance is St Fintan's Well, also known as the 'Wishing Tree'. The nearby original well dried up, but then a spring appeared in a very old tree, in a pocket where the tree branches about six feet from the ground, and there was always water here, even in the height of summer. People venerated the tree, inserting coins into the bark and making wishes. A few decades ago, the tree was blown down in a storm, but for a long time the council workers refused to remove it, for fear of being cursed for life. The tree never died, and eventually the dead trunk was removed, leaving what now looks like a new tree.

Former Infirmary, Dublin Road

In bygone times, people went to the dispensary, which was staffed by a doctor and sometimes a nurse, for their medicines. The dispensary was on Grattan Street in the opening years of the twentieth century, until a new one was built in 1940 to the west of the infirmary on Dublin Road (to the east of the current fire station).

'Infirm' or very sick people went to the infirmary for operations and convalescence. In Portlaoise, the original infirmary was on Church Avenue from 1756, in the charge of Dr Michael Jacob, comprising at least part of the 'Stone House' dating from the sixteenth century. In 1808, Dr John Jacob founded a new infirmary on the Dublin Road, having despaired of the poor conditions in the old one, and the funding was provided by James Grattan, son of the more famous Henry Grattan (as evidenced by the stone plaque inside the hall). The Presentations nuns took over the old infirmary in 1824.

Queen's County Sanatorium (for tuberculosis patients) was built directly behind the infirmary in 1911.

When the infirmary was superseded by the general hospital in 1937, and the TB sanatorium moved to Shaen in 1931, the building lay idle until it was taken over as county council offices and yard space after the Second World War. However, it became redundant after 1982, when the new county council offices were built on JFL Avenue.

In 2001, the site was sold to a developer who built Grattan apartment blocks and refurbished the 1808 infirmary before leasing it as government offices.

Shaen Sanatorium, near Emo

Shaen House was built about 1820 for the Kemmis family, on the site of an earlier house, and for a few decades they operated a big iron foundry from a variety of outbuildings there. The Ordnance Survey map of 1839 shows Shaen Castle in ruins in the woods to the south of the house, which nowadays resembles an abandoned walled garden of early nineteenth-century vintage.

After the death of Captain Thomas Henry Kemmis, the house furniture was auctioned off in 1916. It wasn't until 1928 that the house and 70 acres of the bigger estate was sold to the Health Board, who converted it into Shaen Sanatorium in 1930–31 for the treatment of tuberculosis (TB), which required isolation and plenty of fresh air.

In 1961, Shaen became an outpost of St Fintan's Hospital, for the treatment of elderly patients with dementia.

Some people may recall the early 1970s, when Shaen was used to house refugees from 'the Troubles' in Northern Ireland, mostly children.

Nowadays, Shaen is called St Brigid's Hospital and it is run by the HSE for elderly patients.

Midland Regional Hospital, Dublin Road

The general hospital was built as a replacement for the nearby infirmary, and the foundation stone was laid on 17 December 1936 by the Laoighse County Board of Health & Public Assistance. Architects Scott and Good produced the modern design, and it was built by Collen Bros of Dublin.

The running of the hospital was taken over by the Holy Family Sisters in 1945, but it wasn't until 1954 that a nurses' home-cum-convent was built for them. Initially, the eleven nuns lived with the Presentation Sisters on Church Avenue. The nuns occupied the south wing of the new building beside the hospital, with a link to the detached chapel which was added in 1959.

The Order was founded by a priest in Bordeaux, France, in 1820, and spread to Newbridge in Ireland in 1875 (where they still have schools). The Irish branch also did mission work around the world, especially with leprosy patients in the British colony of Ceylon (now called Sri Lanka).

The nuns stayed for almost fifty years, and now the hospital is run by the Health Services Executive (HSE). Major rear extensions were added after the nuns left. The former nurses' home/convent is now the administration building. Their chapel is an occasional mortuary but is soon to be converted into meeting rooms and offices.

Ridge Cemetery, Ridge Road

This hillock (ridge) was originally part of an ancient road running from Timahoe to Tullamore in Offaly.

The section in Portlaoise has been a burial ground since the seventeenth century, but closed to new burials from 1897 when St Peter & Paul's cemetery (the 'new cemetery') opened on the Stradbally Road.

St Peter & Paul's Cemetery, Stradbally Road

St Peter & Paul's cemetery opened as a Catholic burial ground in 1897, and still has enough space for generations to come.

Noteworthy plots are those of the Presentations nuns, the Holy Family nuns, and the Christian Brothers. St Fintan's Hospital has a plot, including a stone monument erected in 1995, for the numerous unnamed patients who died between 1900 and 1985 (there is another cemetery inside the hospital grounds for earlier burials). The priests of the parish have a circular island plot, but also have a few graves in the grounds of St Peter & Paul's church, including those exhumed from the old church in Church Avenue. The Holy Family Sisters have only three burials here, Mother St John O'Donoghue (1962), and two nuns who died in a car crash in 1979.

During the 1997 conversion of the old gaol into the Dunamaise Arts Centre, the skeletons of eleven former prisoners were found. The remains, which were at least 200 years old, were exhumed and reinterred on 29 November 2001 in the new section of St Peter & Paul's cemetery, with a simple headstone on their plot.

This cemetery must be the most restful place in the country, because it is packed with beautiful modern marble seats dedicated to the families of the deceased.

On the north side, a low wall separates the Protestant section, which was consecrated on 30 March 1899, and comprises a narrow strip of land, with a separate entrance from the road. Other Protestants, including the Jacob medical family, are buried in the very old cemetery in Railway Street, where their original church was located – the ancient tower is still standing. The graveyard around St Peter's church on Grattan Street is still in use.

Poorhouse

Portlaoise never had a workhouse during the Famine years of the mid-nineteenth century, but the 1839 Ordnance Survey map denotes the ruins of a poorhouse immediately to the north of the army barracks (now Garda station), where government offices were built in recent years.

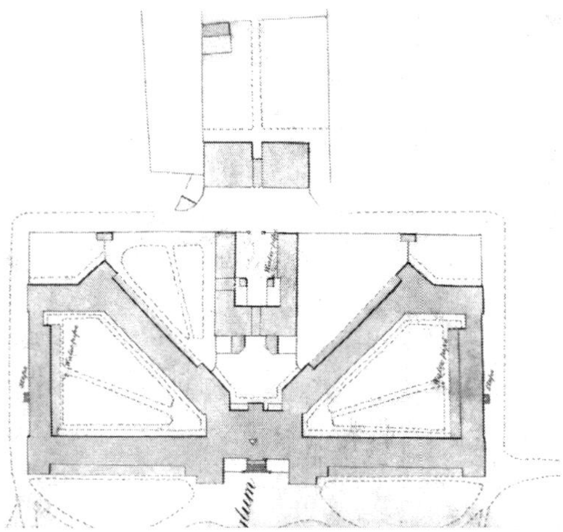

Left: Ordnance Survey plan (1839) of Portlaoise Lunatic Asylum, a few years after it opened in 1833. (*Courtesy of National Archives of Ireland.*)

Below: Ordnance Survey plan (1907) of Portlaoise Lunatic Asylum, with various extensions. Note the county infirmary opposite the convict prison. (Courtesy of Trinity College Dublin.)

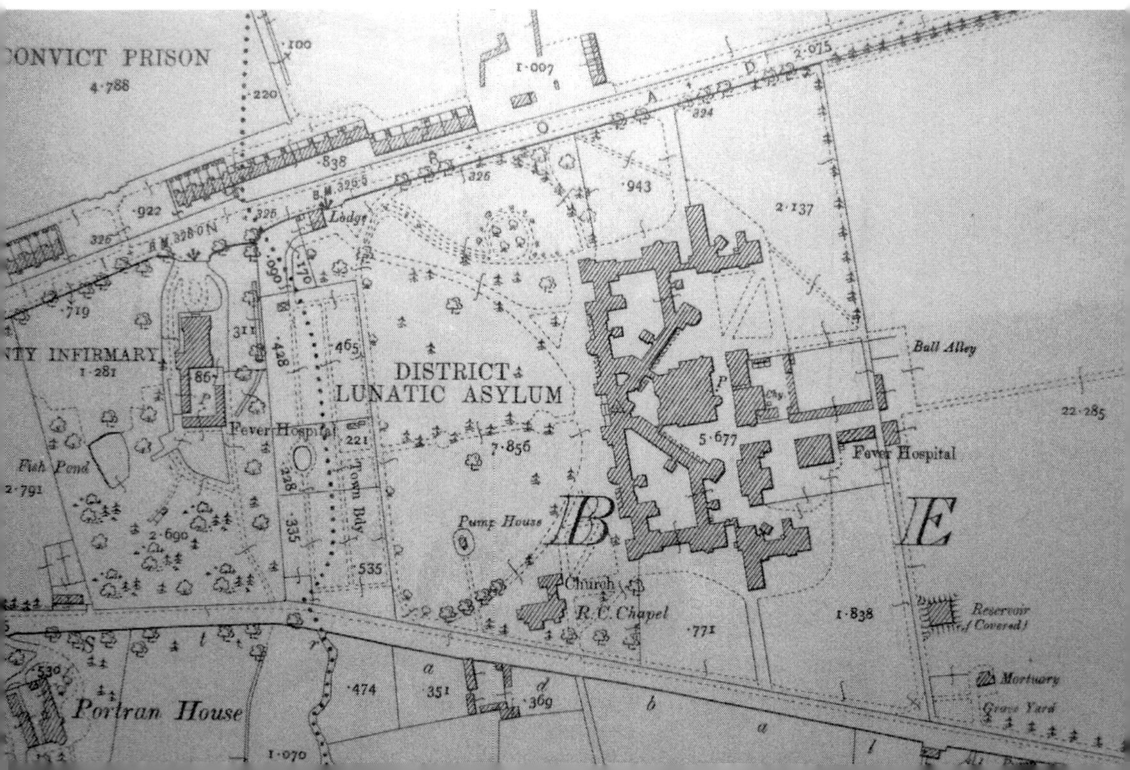

Above: St Fintan's Hospital was originally the Lunatic Asylum, and nowadays it offers a variety of supports for mental health problems.

Below: The central block of St Fintan's Hospital was originally the Governor's residence.

Later extensions to St Fintan's Hospital employed red brick to enliven the buildings.

St Fintan's Hospital has two places of worship for patients and staff, Catholic on the left and Anglican on the right, linked by the two doors and a shared mortuary.

The Catholic chapel in St Fintan's Hospital has three lovely Harry Clarke stained-glass windows.

St Fintan's Hospital erected a very sad and lonely monument in recent years in memory of the hundreds (probably more) of unnamed Christians who were buried in this hidden mass grave from 1833 to 1896.

The twenty-three-bed St Brigid's Hospital was originally Shaen Tuberculosis Sanatorium in the 1940s, and it was later linked to St Fintan's Hospital.

The impressive but unbalanced entrance to Shaen Hospital replaced the original gate lodge, probably in the early nineteenth century.

The former county infirmary is now part of Grattan Business Park, a mixture of offices and new apartments. (*Courtesy of Laois Local Studies – Scully Collection.*)

Aerial view of the Midlands Regional Hospital, which is now much larger. The detached block at the rear was the nurses' home (rooms for nurses) and Nuns' convent, plus a side chapel. (*Courtesy of Midland Regional Hospital.*)

Current view of part of the Midlands Regional Hospital.

The Midlands Hospital uses the former nurses' home and convent as offices.

The unique Ridge cemetery has potential as a tourist attraction.

This sad monument was erected in Portlaoise cemetery in recent years to commemorate hundreds of unnamed Christian patients from St Fintan's Hospital who died over the past century.

The Presentation nuns from Church Avenue cemetery were reinterred in this new plot in Portlaoise cemetery in recent years.

Above left: The Christian Brothers have their own plot in Portlaoise cemetery.

Above right: The very old St Fintan's Well, Clonenagh, Mountrath, also known as the 'Wishing Tree', has sprung to life again after having been blown down in a bad storm a few decades ago.

FOUR

Business

Mince Norton (Maryborough Maltings), Coote Street

The process of malting barley was a long and laborious one. Throughout the autumn, farmers brought their loads of barley into the yard via the gap between the big red-brick house and the malt houses, where it was weighed, checked and stored in the barley lofts. This raw barley was then partially dried in the kiln, by being spread out on the perforated tiled floor of the kiln to a depth of 10 inches – the coal-fired boilers/furnace underneath provided the hot air. During the drying, the barley was hand-turned by the workmen.

The dried barley was screened for waste, and dropped into ground-level water-filled 'steeps', starting the germination process. The wet and growing barley was then spread out on the malthouse floor, and after a few days was shovelled up by the men through trapdoors onto the floor above, spread out again, and finally shovelled up onto the top floor.

In order to stop the germinating barley converting the starch into sugar, it was brought to the kiln and dried out completely over four days, being turned over by the men every six hours, thus causing the 'combings' or shoots to fall off. The malted barley was then transferred to malt bins, screened, and finally transferred to sacks for transport by Guinness trucks to their brewery in Dublin.

The introduction of conveyors and mechanical shovels after the Second World War did away with most of the back-breaking labour, likewise the installation of two 21ft-high cylindrical steel 'steeps' or 'aerators', and the conversion to oil for the kilns in 1951. In the old days, about thirty men were employed, but this was reduced to about ten after mechanisation, although additional men were employed during the autumn harvest.

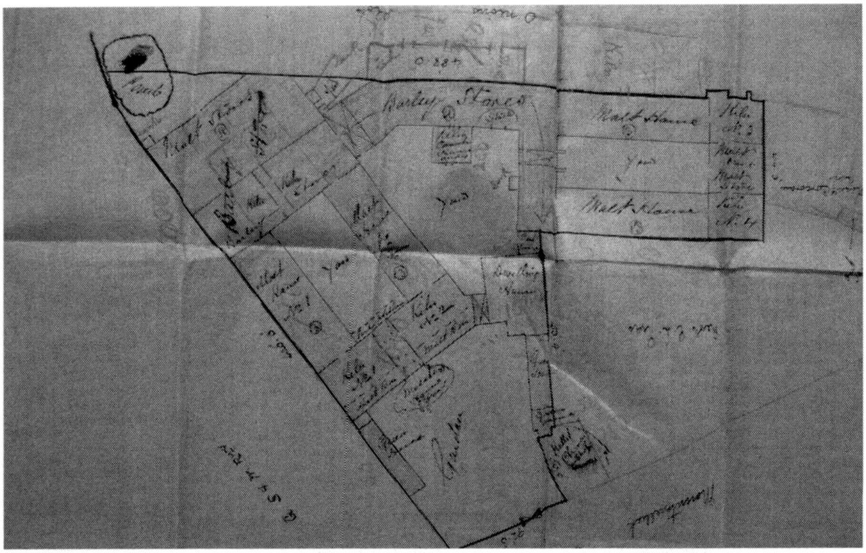

Layout of Maryboro Maltings, Coote Street, 1887. (*Courtesy of National Archives of Ireland.*)

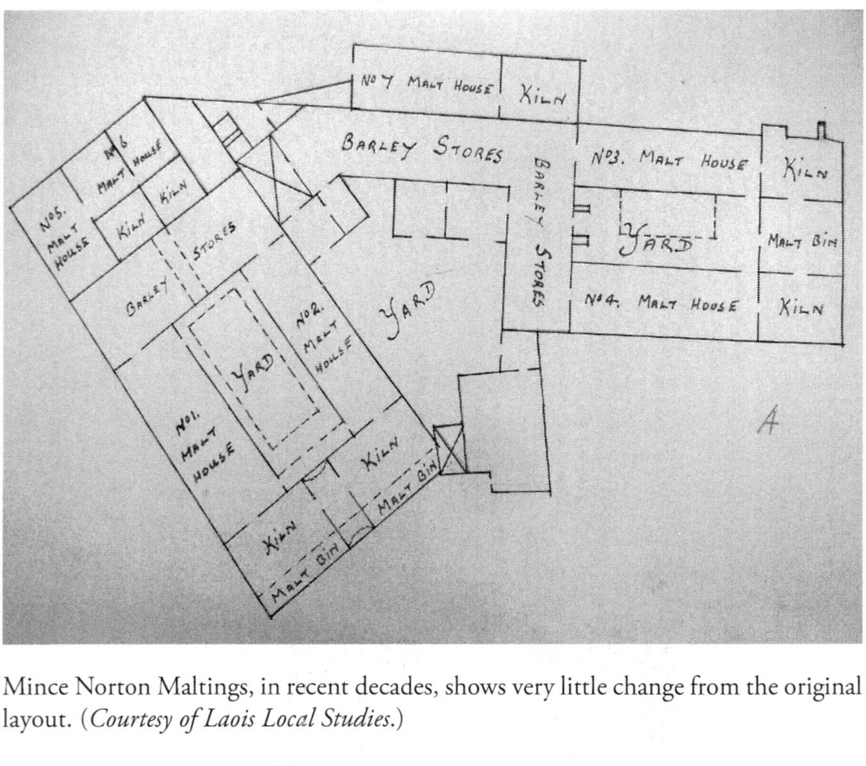

Mince Norton Maltings, in recent decades, shows very little change from the original layout. (*Courtesy of Laois Local Studies.*)

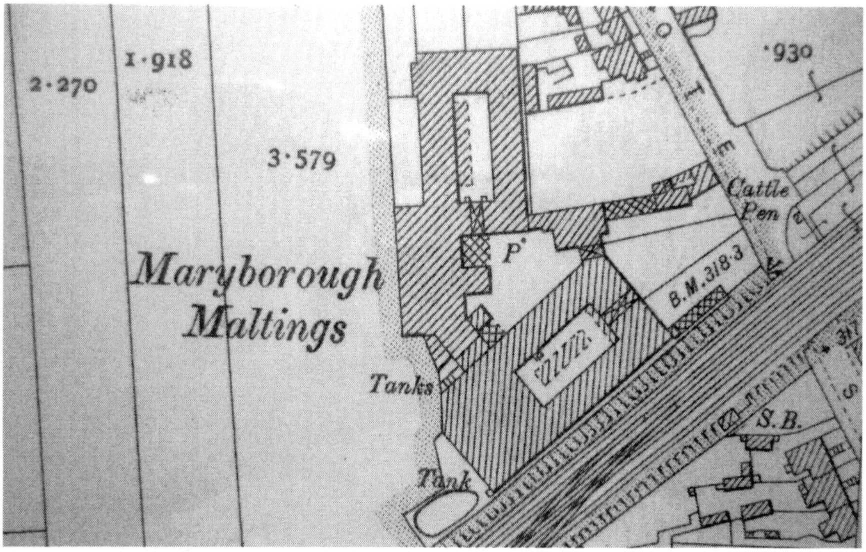

Ordnance Survey plan (1907) of Maryborough Maltings, Coote Street. Note the cattle pen beside the railway. (*Courtesy of Trinity College Dublin.*)

In 1856, the Great Southern & Western Railway leased 3½ acres of land to Thomas Turpin, and in 1866 he leased 1½ acres of that land to John Wrafter, who built a malting works that same year. The Bank of Ireland foreclosed on a mortgage in 1886 and sold the business to Robert Gibney. He died in 1911, and the executor of his will was Joseph Tyrrell, whose family took an active part in the business after that, with the company being called Roche Gibney in the 1970s. Mince Norton took over the business from 1979, but only used the buildings for drying and storing the barley, which would then be malted in their fully mechanised Athy maltings.

Matthew Mince, a farmer from Portersize, Ballitore, County Kildare, had started a malting business in 1848 in Athy. In 1921, Mince merged with P.R. Norton, creating Mince Norton, and from 1959 it was was a fully mechanised business needing only a small workforce. The company is now called Mince Malt and is still based in Athy.

Greencore sold the Portlaoise premises in 2003, and the site now awaits redevelopment. Most of the malt buildings have been demolished, except the 1866 front wall, with two kilns and malt bins behind it. The 1880 red-brick house is now a separate private business and features some nice internal plasterwork. A smaller nearby house has also survived.

A schedule of the seven 3-storey buildings in Portlaoise was prepared in 1904 for submission to Guinness (a major purchaser of malted barley for their stout), comprising the following:

> House 1 and 2 were the same: 124ft long by 30ft wide, each with two 'steeps', and each having a kiln, 48ft by 25ft.
>
> House 3 and 4 were the same: 142ft by 30ft, each with a kiln of 40ft by 30ft.
>
> House 5 and 6 were the same: 84ft by 26ft, each with a kiln, 25ft by 25ft.
>
> House 7 was 82ft by 30ft, with a kiln of 42ft by 30ft.

In the seven kilns, the height from the kiln spars to the tiles averaged 12ft.

Mince Norton in recent decades. Farmers brought their barley through the gap beside the manager's fine house. (*Courtesy of Laois Local Studies – Scully Collection.*)

Aerial photo of Mince Norton in the 1950s. (*Courtesy of National Library.*)

Mince Norton looking from the courtyard towards Coote Street, with kilns on both sides of archway. (*Courtesy of Laois Local Studies.*)

Mince Norton courtyard, looking west. (*Courtesy of Laois Local Studies.*)

Mince Norton barley propagation floor. (*Courtesy of Laois Local Studies.*)

Mince Norton distribution ductwork. (*Courtesy of Laois Local Studies.*)

Mince Norton attic floor. (*Courtesy of Laois Local Studies.*)

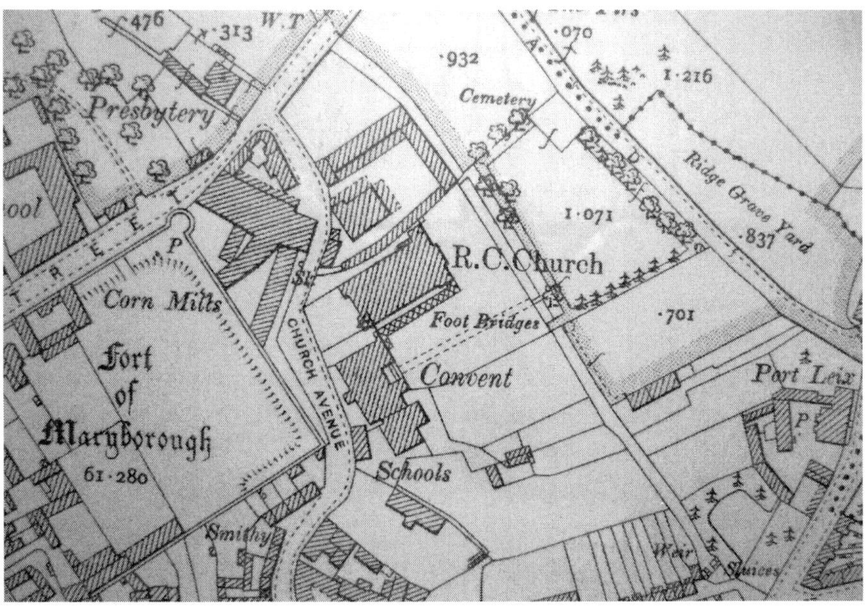

Ordnance Survey map (1907) showing Odlums Flour Mills (corn flour). (*Courtesy of Trinity College Dublin.*)

Irish Worsted Mills Ltd, Old Knockmay Road, off Grattan Street

Worsteds are good-quality wool products. The company produced ladies' and gents' suits, making the cloth in the factory and employing such skilled trades as weavers, warpers, pickers and menders.

The company was founded and owned by Pepper Lee & Co. Ltd, 7 Nelson Street, Bradford, Yorkshire, England. In 1936, thirty-two schoolgirls and two schoolboys from the technical school were sent over to Bradford to train in the business of weaving and so on, with Catholic Church supervision regarding accommodation, etc. The Portlaoise site was donated by local businessman Mr V.G. Hinds, and the new factory was built in 1936–37 by Farmer Bros of Dublin, with structural steel by Thompson of Carlow. Extensions were added between 1946 and 1950. A branch railway line ran into the site.

The company was the biggest in Portlaoise, employing hundreds of workers in its heyday, and its staff enjoyed a good social life, with their own drama society, choir, and football and camogie teams.

Sadly, the company closed in November 1972, with the loss of about 160 jobs. Eir, a telecommunications company, now occupies the building.

W. P. & R. Odlum, Church Avenue

This famous flour-manufacturing company, with its iconic owl logo, was started by the Odlum family in Portlaoise in 1845, initially leasing the refurbished three-storey flour mill (shown on an 1823 map) from William Kelly. William Perry Odlum (W.P.) and Richard Odlum (R.) took over the business in due course.

Wheat was traditionally ground into flour by crushing it between one fixed horizontal and one rotating circular stone, together called a 'pair of stones'. Big mills needed many 'pairs'. The motive power came from the big waterwheel, fed from a 'head-race' or canal taken off the River Triogue, or fed from stored water in the mill pond (for summer use, when the river might dry up). In the 1850s, the 'breast' waterwheel was 17ft diameter, and 6½ft wide, providing 12-15HP (horsepower), driving five pairs of stones, 4ft 4 inches in diameter. There was also a steam-powered mill on the other side of the road, driving three pairs of stones. Rollers replaced grinding stones in 1887.

Many people still remember the pond and head race on Church Avenue, in front of the Catholic church and the Presentation Convent.

Odlums Flour Mill in recent decades, with 1930s grain storage silos on the site of the former Mill Pond. (*Courtesy of Laois Local Studies – Scully Collection.*)

Flour mills tend to be very dry and dusty, and so following a serious fire in 1909, the mill was completely rebuilt in 1911.

The 1930s saw the installation of a battery of eighteen tall stainless-steel grain-storage silos.

The Portlaoise mill closed in 1977, by which stage it dominated and towered over both sides of the north end of Church Avenue, and it was demolished in 1991, except for a low building inside the old fort walls abutting the bastion. Odlums still have their big mill in Portarlington, occupying a much more suitable site near the railway station, and it has a battery of silos of the same vintage as those in Portlaoise. They also still own a big mill on Alexandra Road in the Dublin Docklands.

The Fitzmaurice Plaza and Lawn is now on the western half of the site of the Odlum's flour mill and pond. This choice of name is regrettable, since Odlums is of national importance, and provided major employment for Portlaoise people for 130 years, surely meriting a memorial.

The Odlum family also owned Meelick Mills, with its 18ft waterwheel, and the three-storey Green Mills, with a 16ft waterwheel, from the 1860s to around 1908. One of the Odlum family lived in 'Woodville', Meelick, which was once a private asylum run by Dr Jacob called the Midland Retreat.

Aerial photos of Church Avenue from the 1950s, showing how Odlums Flour Mill dominated the church and convent. (*Courtesy of Laois Local Studies.*)

Fitzmaurice Plaza now occupies the site of the former Odlums Flour Mill.

Swedish-owned Tretorn tennis-ball factory, pictured in 1996. (*Courtesy of Laois Local Studies.*)

Opposite page:

Above: Aerial photo of Irish Worsted Mills in the 1950s. (*Courtesy of National Library.*)

Centre: The former Irish Worsted Mills building, with extensions built over the decades, is now occupied by Eir.

Below: Irish Worsted Mills provided many skilled jobs. (*Courtesy of Laois Local Studies.*)

Another section of Irish Worsteds Mills. (*Courtesy of Laois Local Studies – John O'Brien Collection.*)

Some staff of Irish Worsteds Mills. (*Courtesy of Laois Local Studies – John O'Brien Collection.*)

Irish Worsteds Mills had its own musical society. (*Courtesy of Laois Local Studies – John O'Brien Collection.*)

The annual outing from Irish Worsteds Mills was a big social occasion for the staff. (*Courtesy of John O'Brien Collection – Laois Local Studies.*)

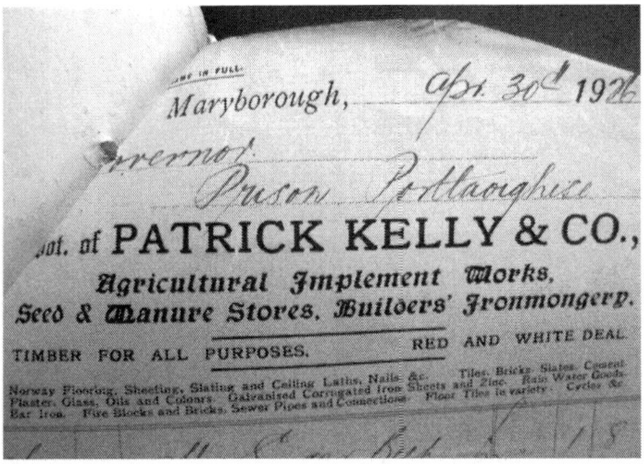

Left: A 1926 invoice from Patrick Kelly & Co., who were famous throughout Ireland for their good-value hay sheds. (*Courtesy of National Archives of Ireland.*)

Below: Patrick Kelly had extensive ironworks behind the Methodist church on Railway Street. (*Courtesy of Laois Local Studies.*)

Kelly's Hay Barns, Railway Street

Murdoch Campbell founded Agricultural Implement Manufacturers & Manure Merchants in 1870, and in 1878 Patrick Kelly & Co. took over. The company made all sorts of farm machinery but is probably best remembered for its iconic haybarn. The simple steel design, ease of erection, durability, and reasonable price made it famous throughout Ireland, and thousands are still in use, with the nameplate of white letters on a blue background.

In the 1960s the company employed 250 people, and had 120,000 square feet of workshops and stores between Coote Street and Railway Street.

The company closed in 1984, with the loss of thirty-five jobs. The big site was redeveloped as the enormous Heritage Hotel in 2003, which has since been renamed the Midland Park Hotel.

Tretorn Sport Ltd, JFL Avenue

This Swedish company, which made tennis balls, opened in 1973 on the Kylekiproe Industrial Estate. The low factory was designed by Michael Scott & Partners, and built by Walls of Dublin.

The factory closed in 2004 with the loss of 68 jobs (there were around 130 employees in 1988 and 90 in 1996). The German-owned Aldi built a discount supermarket on the site in 2006.

Gasworks, Well Road

Nowadays we take instant electricity for granted, but 'town gas' was used throughout Ireland in the nineteenth and twentieth centuries for lighting, cooking and heating, with each town having its own manufacturing plant. The gas was manufactured by burning bituminous coal in 'retorts', and storing the resulting gas in big metal cylinders called 'gasometers', before being distributed around the town in underground pipes. Portlaoise had a gas plant from at least 1857, situated on the Well Road. Electricity for the town's needs crept in during the early decades of the twentieth century, and the gas plant closed in 1932. Later, the Macra na Feirme (Young Farmers' Club) hall was built on the site, and it is still in use today. In recent decades, 'natural' gas from the Kinsale field off the south coast of Ireland has been piped around Ireland and used for cooking and central heating in homes.

Banks

The big house at the north-west corner of Church Street, where it joins Railway Street, was the Bank of Ireland from around 1850, but is now empty.

The refreshing red-bricked Munster & Leinster Bank, 17 Main Street, was built in 1891, including the manager's house attached to its right side. It became AIB (Allied Irish Bank) in 1966 but is now in other commercial use.

Hotels

The main hotel in Portlaoise from the 1890s to the 1970s was Kelly's Hotel, on Main Street opposite Church Street. It was originally called the Hibernian Hotel, and this name can still be seen at the top of the plastered façade.

Aird's Central Hotel was at 30 Main Street from about 1904 to the 1960s, then Henderson's, and now O'Loughlin's Hotel.

Egan's Hostelry was at 25/24 Main Street from 1929 until about 2015, operating as a café initially and then a restaurant. Now, Lilly's operates a similar business in the spacious premises.

Nowadays, the Midland Park Hotel (built in 2003 as the Heritage Hotel), off Coote Street, caters for tourists and conferences, and likewise the slightly older Killeshin Hotel on the Dublin Road.

Post Office

On the 1839 Ordnance Survey map, a post office is shown on the south side of Lower Main Street. A new three-storey post office was built in 1910 on the opposite side of the road, at 27 Main Street. From 1972 to 1994, a modern office building on Coote Street (east of St Peter's church) housed the post office, but now it is in modern premises (built in the 1980s) in Lyster Square.

These days, Portlaoise has a huge mail sorting office off the Abbeyleix Road, in the Clonminam Business Park, second only to Dublin's in size, and it acts as a central hub for the entire country.

Leinster Express, 107 Lower Main Street

This famous newspaper was founded in 1831 by Henry Talbot, and was based at the corner of Market Square and Coote Street from 1850 to 1970s.

Shaws, JFL Avenue

Shaws drapery shop was founded in Mountmellick in 1864, expanding into a department store in later years, and it still has branches throughout Ireland, run by the Shaw family. The Portlaoise branch is one of the best-loved stores in the town, being based since 1890 at 23 Main Street, at the corner of Church Avenue. In 2013, it moved to the new shopping district on the south side of the town. The county council has plans to build a public library on the old Shaws site, despite the fact that the courthouse would be more appropriate for a civic amenity (the court would be better situated beside the Garda station).

Córas Iompair Éireann

Portlaoise is situated in the centre of Ireland, and so Córas Iompair Éireann (CIÉ) has a Traincare Depot at Knockmay for servicing trains. It also has a sleeper and track depot for stockholding the iron tracks and concrete sleepers required for the rail network.

eir (was Eircom), Old Knockmay Road

The telecommunications company occupies the former premises of Irish Worsted Mills.

Telfords, Clonminam Business Park

Telfords is a household name in the midlands, being a major builders' provider and DIY retailer. The company was founded in Mountrath in 1885, where it's still going strong. It is a one-stop shop for farmers and also for housewives up until 1970, since it also had a grocery and bakery section.

Telfords expanded to Portlaoise in 1993, when they acquired their present site from IAWS, and since then have enlarged the business, and are now part of the Grafton Group (which includes Woodie's and Chadwicks). There was also a branch in Athy from 1998 to 2012.

The station master's charming limestone house at Portlaoise Railway Station.

Portlaoise south platform, and disused iron footbridge.

Kilbricken Railway Station, serving Mountrath, is now closed.

Car designs and fashions evolve, but Main Street never seems to change. (*Courtesy of Redmonds Photography, Roscrea.*)

Shaws Department Store has moved to the new shopping quarter near County Hall. Their former shop would make a great hotel or musical 'watering hole'.

Lower Main Street still has the red-bricked former Munster & Leinster Bank.

Upper Main Street seems to have lost some of its character. (*Image below courtesy of Redmonds Photography, Roscrea.*)

This Lower Main Street landmark was typical of rural pubs, with the grocery shop on one side and the bar on the other.

Market Square encompasses a triangle, a circle, and The Square Bar (Fitzpatrick's).

Glanbia Agribusiness, Clonminam Business Park

This modern mill processes grains and seeds, and produces animal feed on a large scale.

Department of Agriculture, Abbeyleix Road

The government offices beside the Garda station are housed in a modern building.

Maryborough Coach Factory

Most people have probably forgotten this prestigious enterprise, which catered for horse-drawn transport needs before the automobile took over. From about 1895 to 1911, William Crennan built coaches, and he was also a house painter.

Tannery

An 'Old Tannery', south of Lower Main Street on Pepper Lane, is shown on the 1839 Ordnance Survey map, and another tannery is also shown south of the convent school. There was also a tannery long ago on Tea Lane, off Grattan Street.

Railway

The coming of the Great Southern & Western Railway Company in 1847 ushered in an era of prosperity for the town, allowing goods and supplies, including cattle and coal, to flow in and out at great speed. The cattle pen was accessed from Coote Street. The station cost the enormous amount of £2,000, comprising refreshment rooms, first-class waiting rooms, third-class waiting room, ticket office, station master's apartment, and a goods station. Initially, the refreshment rooms were managed by Hotel Maryborough, on the condition that all trains stop for ten to fifteen minutes, based on eight trains daily on weekdays, and four on Sunday.

The train track and the station are located on a high embankment, with the two-storey station master's house alongside. The design and workmanship of the limestone buildings is exceptional, far superior to anything else in the town. Two iron footbridges over the tracks were erected in 1890, but one has disappeared and the other is closed, and has been replaced by a very plain modern bridge.

Mountrath was served by the attractive station at Kilbricken, which was also built in 1847, but it was closed a few decades ago.

FIVE

Law & Order

Portlaoise Prison, Dublin Road

The old L-shaped Maryborough Gaol on Church Street was directly behind the present courthouse, and was built in 1789, its beautiful limestone façade belying its purpose. The Government Inspector's Report for 1823 stated that the gaol could hold ninety prisoners (male and female) but was in poor condition. In that year, there were visiting Anglican and Catholic chaplains, each paid £30 a year, and a schoolmaster, paid £40. After the new gaol was built on the Dublin Road in 1830, the old gaol was used for various official activities, especially as a county council public library during most of the twentieth century.

In 1997, during conversion of the former gaol into the Dunamaise Arts Centre, eleven human skeletons were found, and in 2001 were reinterred (beside the Aird marble seat) in the new section of St Peter & Paul's cemetery under a simple headstone. The skeletons are estimated to be at least 200 years old.

The new Maryborough Gaol opened in 1830 and was built with ashlar limestone to a common design, comprising a three-storey castellated central block with four radiating wings. The governor lived in the central block, which also accommodated the gaol kitchen, shared chapel, and boardroom. The wings contained eight wards, four for male criminals, two for male debtors, one for female criminals, and one for female debtors. About 30 acres of adjacent land was acquired towards the end of the century for use as a farm.

The Government Reports for the 1830s on the new Maryborough Gaol recorded that there were on average 130-150 prisoners (male and female), 87 cells, and a small infirmary. Most of the men were occupied making cloth on the eleven looms, tailoring, shoemaking, or working in the forge, while the women did washing and cleaning. The 15-manpower treadmill was for those given a sentence of hard labour, and this was used to pump water from their own reservoir, fed from a small stream passing through the site. The treadmill was housed in a building 35ft by 19ft, by 16ft high, with two small sheds alongside.

The Government Reports in the mid-1840s, just before the Famine, do not record any increase in the convict population. Turnkeys (warders) ran the school, and Dr John Jacob was in charge of the gaol infirmary. Some of the prisoners were paid for the products they made. The Report for 1846 records ninety-nine prisoners, including seven debtors and fourteen 'lunatics', accommodated in ninety-five cells, ten day rooms, eight yards, eight solitary cells for punishment, the infirmary, shared chapel, kitchen, laundry, etc. However, the prisoners did not engage in any trades and were idle, which was not always the case. Meals were taken in the cells, and a regime of silence was enforced throughout the prison at all times. Baths were used only on entering the prison for delousing, and then the prisoners used tubs to wash themselves. Sometimes the sewers worked, while cesspits were used at other times.

By 1849, the prison population averaged 250-300 on any one day, no doubt occasioned by the Famine.

The Government Report for the year ending March 1902 recorded the prisoners working as tailors, shoemakers, bookbinders, or on the 30-acre farm, and being paid around 12*d* to 17*d* per day, depending on skill. Others were paid to work inside the prison, cleaning, mending clothes, washing, and cooking, or as carpenters and smiths.

After Irish independence in 1922, and right up to the 1970s, the prisoners continued to work on the farm, which specialised in vegetables and pigs. This was very therapeutic work; some of the produce was used for their own needs, and the rest was sold to the public, resulting in good profits, especially on the pigs, potatoes and cabbage. Produce sold included cabbage, carrots, parsnips, cauliflowers, celery, parsley, currants, grapes, onions, leeks, peas, beans, potatoes, rhubarb, seakale, strawberries, tomatoes and turnips, as well as oats and hay. The pigsties were to the east of the prison buildings, alongside the Dublin Road.

Unlike St Fintan's Hospital across the road, the prison did not have a cemetery. However, two men who were executed in 1941–42 (during the 'Emergency') were buried in the prison grounds, but were exhumed and moved to a cemetery in County Louth in 1948.

The prison has been modernised, altered and extended over the years, and the last south-east radiating wing was demolished in 2018. Luckily, the elaborate and finely detailed three-storey governor's house has not been demolished. Now called 'The Castle' and used as offices, it should be designated a protected structure or national monument. A separate governor's residence had been built in the south-west corner of the campus in the closing decades of the nineteenth century, but it was recently demolished.

Originally, the upper floor of the iconic stone entrance block was used as a residence by one of the high-ranking staff, but nowadays this entrance is not used, and the two modern bungalows at the roadside for security checks have gone. The long, detached four-storey E-Block along the east side of the prison was built between 1898 and 1902, and is still in use for prisoners' cells. There were thirty-three attractive prison officers' houses built alongside the Dublin Road around 1900 – some two storey, others single storey with a projecting porch – but all were demolished around 1981. Nowadays, the prison is maximum security, with army patrols inside, and houses on average about 250 male prisoners at any one time.

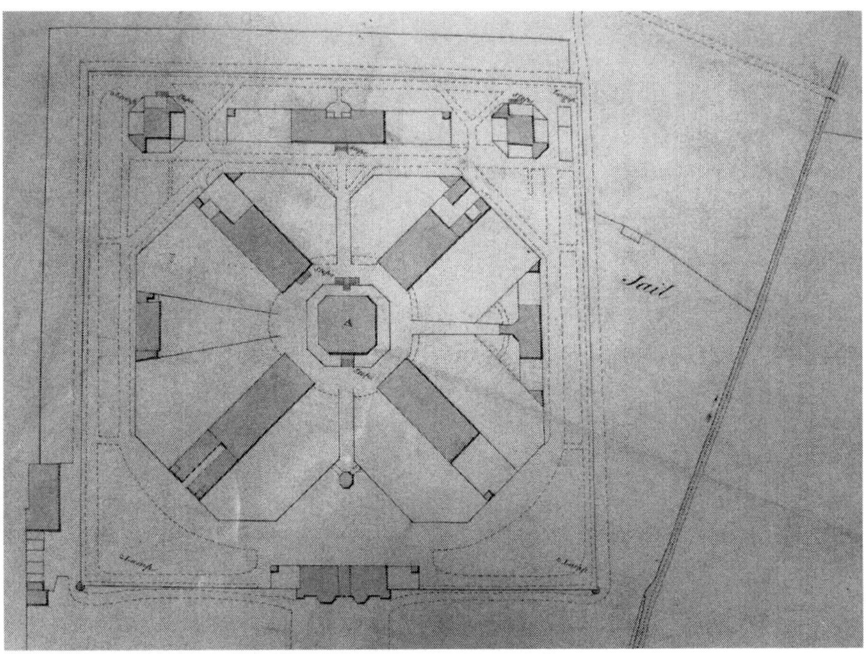

Ordnance Survey plan (1839) of Maryborough (Portlaoise) Prison, with the governor's residence in the centre. (*Courtesy of National Archives of Ireland.*)

A very recent addition to the prison comprises a memorial in the lawn alongside the Dublin Road, to commemorate all prison staff who served since the foundation in 1830. Around 1880, a detached Catholic chapel was built to the north of the governor's central block, but this was demolished in recent decades. Some limestone tracery from the west-facing three-light window of the chapel (which had stained glass by Mayer of Munich at one stage) is now incorporated into the new memorial, and the chapel bell is hung on a new steel frame. The inscriptions on the refurbished bell (minus clapper) include the date, 1830, and the foundry, William Dobson of Downham, Norfolk, England. This bell was probably in the clock tower on top of the central governor's block, since the chapel was originally in this building, and the bell may also have been used for hour-striking.

Midland Prison, Dublin Road

This medium-security prison opened in 2000, and adjoins the east side of Portlaoise Prison, occupying what was previously its farm. The building has four radiating wings, and a front U-shaped block, not unlike the 1830s design for the original Maryborough Gaol. At present, about 850 male prisoners are accommodated.

Portlaoise Prison today. The 1830 clock-tower building was originally the central governor's block. The 1902 E-block is on the right.

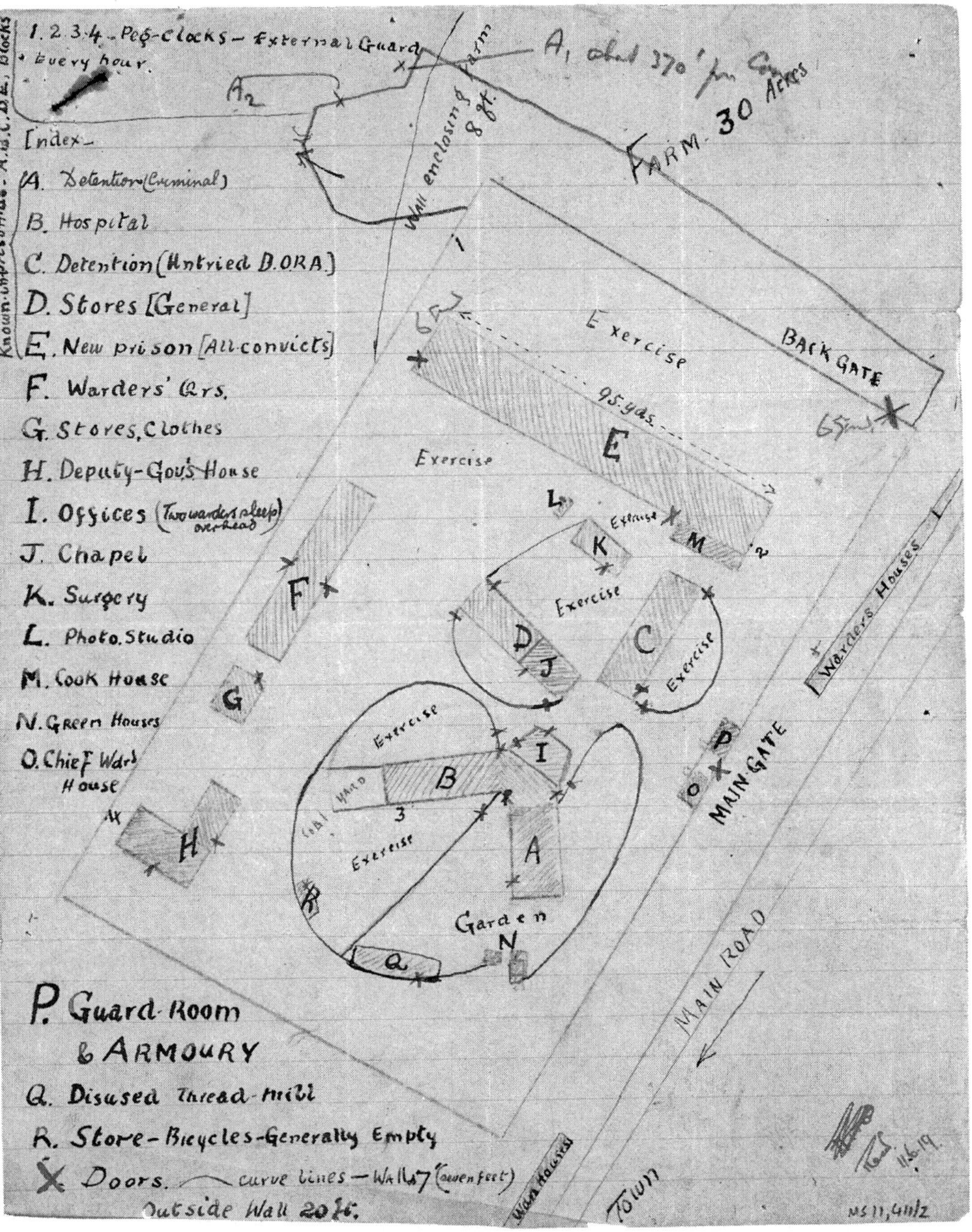

Rough map of Maryborough Prison prepared by Rory O'Connor for a planned breakout in 1919. 'I' is actually much larger, as it was the original central governor's block, and is still used today as offices, with the clock on top. (*Courtesy of National Library of Ireland.*)

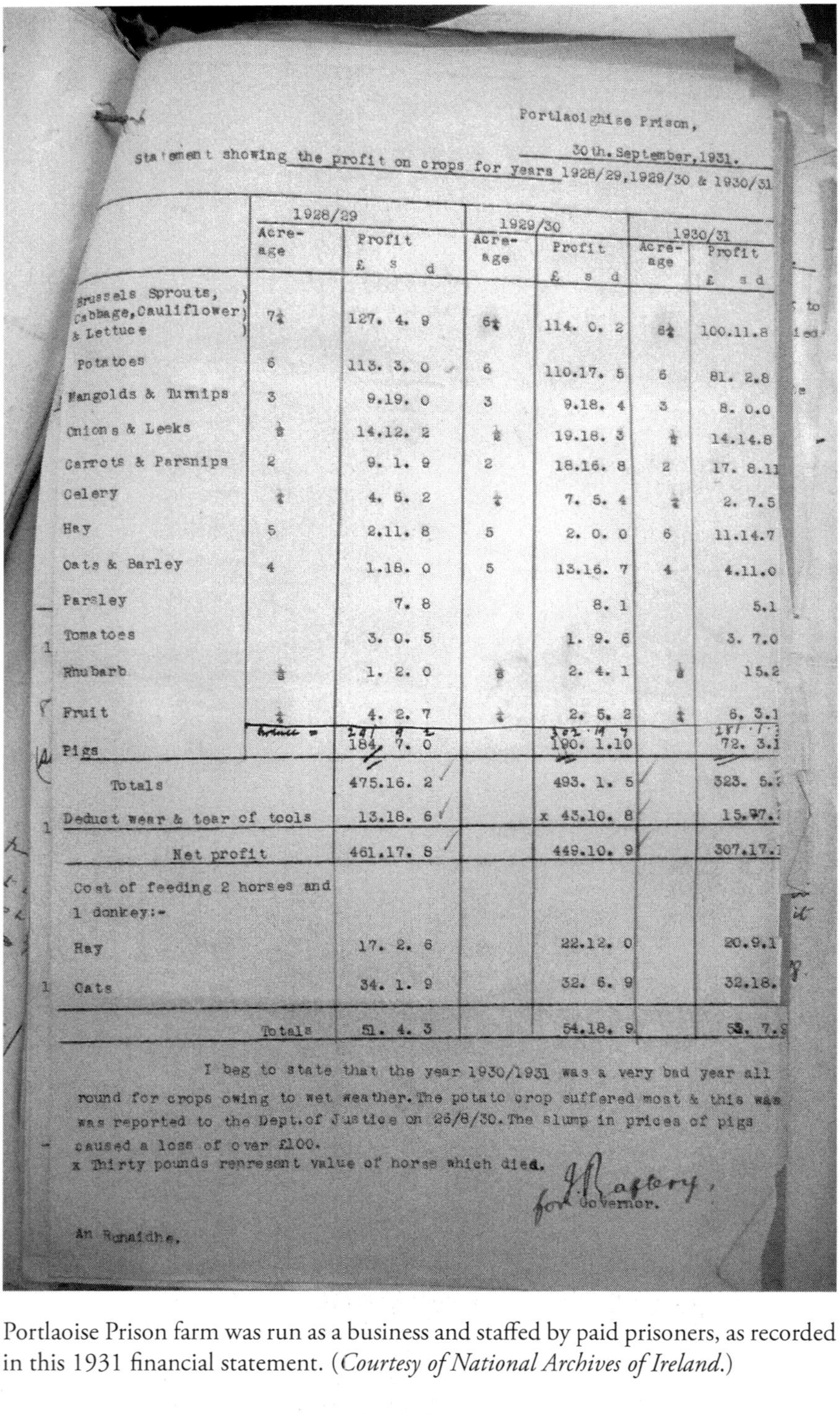

Portlaoighise Prison,

30th. September, 1931.

Statement showing the profit on crops for years 1928/29, 1929/30 & 1930/31

	1928/29		1929/30		1930/31	
	Acreage	Profit £ s d	Acreage	Profit £ s d	Acreage	Profit £ s d
Brussels Sprouts, Cabbage, Cauliflower & Lettuce	7¼	127. 4. 9	6¼	114. 0. 2	6¼	100.11.8
Potatoes	6	113. 3. 0	6	110.17. 5	6	81. 2.8
Mangolds & Turnips	3	9.19. 0	3	9.18. 4	3	8. 0.0
Onions & Leeks	½	14.12. 2	½	19.18. 3	½	14.14.8
Carrots & Parsnips	2	9. 1. 9	2	18.16. 8	2	17. 8.11
Celery	¼	4. 6. 2	¼	7. 5. 4	¼	2. 7.5
Hay	5	2.11. 8	5	2. 0. 0	6	11.14.7
Oats & Barley	4	1.18. 0	5	13.16. 7	4	4.11.0
Parsley		7. 8		8. 1		5.1
Tomatoes		3. 0. 5		1. 9. 6		3. 7.0
Rhubarb	⅛	1. 2. 0	⅛	2. 4. 1	⅛	15.2
Fruit	¼	4. 2. 7	¼	2. 5. 2	¼	6. 3.1
Pigs		184. 7. 0		190. 1.10		72. 3.1
Totals		475.16. 2		493. 1. 5		323. 5.[illegible]
Deduct wear & tear of tools		13.18. 6		x 43.10. 8		15.[illegible]
Net profit		461.17. 8		449.10. 9		307.17.[illegible]
Cost of feeding 2 horses and 1 donkey:-						
Hay		17. 2. 6		22.12. 0		20.9.1
Oats		34. 1. 9		32. 6. 9		32.18.[illegible]
Totals		51. 4. 3		54.18. 9		53. 7.[illegible]

I beg to state that the year 1930/1931 was a very bad year all round for crops owing to wet weather. The potato crop suffered most & this was was reported to the Dept. of Justice on 26/8/30. The slump in prices of pigs caused a loss of over £100.

x Thirty pounds represent value of horse which died.

J. Raftery,
for Governor.

An Rúnaidhe.

Portlaoise Prison farm was run as a business and staffed by paid prisoners, as recorded in this 1931 financial statement. (*Courtesy of National Archives of Ireland.*)

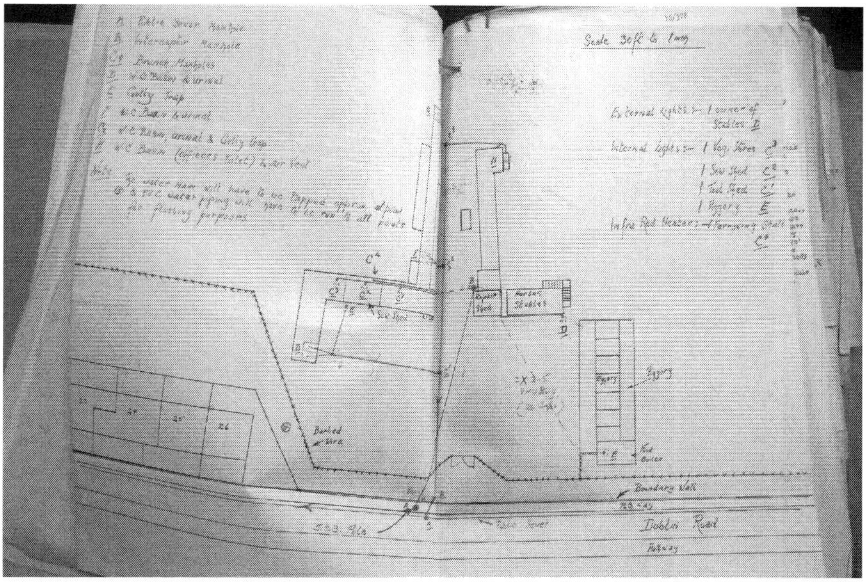

Layout of pigsties on Portlaoise Prison farm, abutting the Dublin Road, just east of the warders' cottages. (*Courtesy of National Archives of Ireland.*)

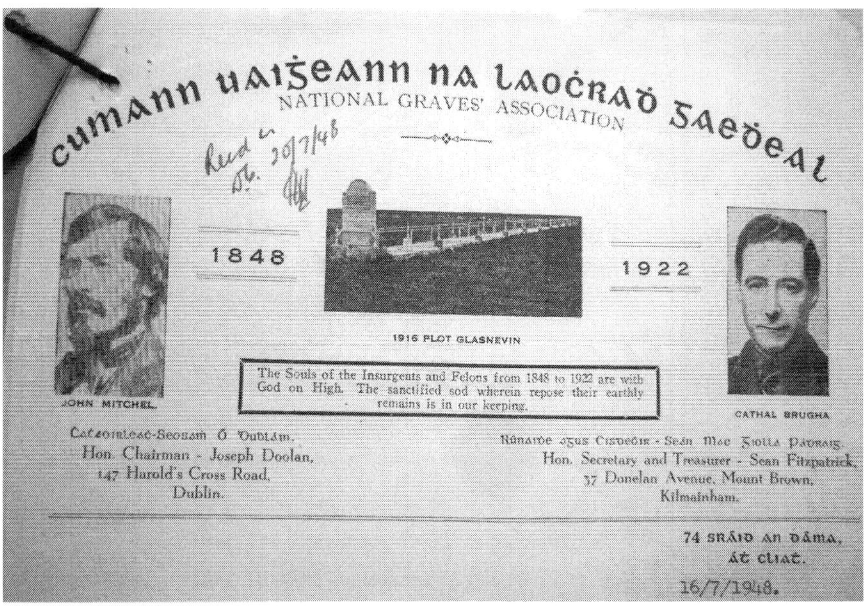

In the 1940s, the National Graves Association campaigned for two prisoners' bodies to be exhumed and reburied elsewhere. (*Courtesy of National Archives.*)

This 2019 memorial honours all those who worked in the prison since 1830, and features part of the chapel window tracery and an 1830 bell.

The 1808 Garda station building was originally a British Army barracks, until 1922.

Most people never see the inside of the iconic 1832 archway leading into the Garda station. In the British Army days, the right-hand building was the guard house and cells, while the left-hand building was the engine house.

Ordnance Survey map (1839) showing the courthouse, the L-shaped old gaol behind, and prison police barracks opposite. (*Courtesy of National Archives.*)

The courthouse in the days when it also served as council offices, with hideous attic extensions. Note Kelly's Hotel and kerbside petrol pump. (*Courtesy of Redmonds Photography, Roscrea.*)

The present courthouse would make a wonderful concert venue-cum-arts centre, with the public library in the former gaol behind, if the courts moved over to the Garda station or the adjoining government offices.

The Dunamaise Arts Centre was originally the gaol, then later council offices.

This fabulous carved stone panel over the entrance to the Dunamaise Arts Centre has all the symbols of law and order, from the scales of justice to the chains of bondage.

The machine shed on the Heath Golf Course has some remains of the former RIC barracks, including a tiny wing which seems to have been an observation post or holding cell.

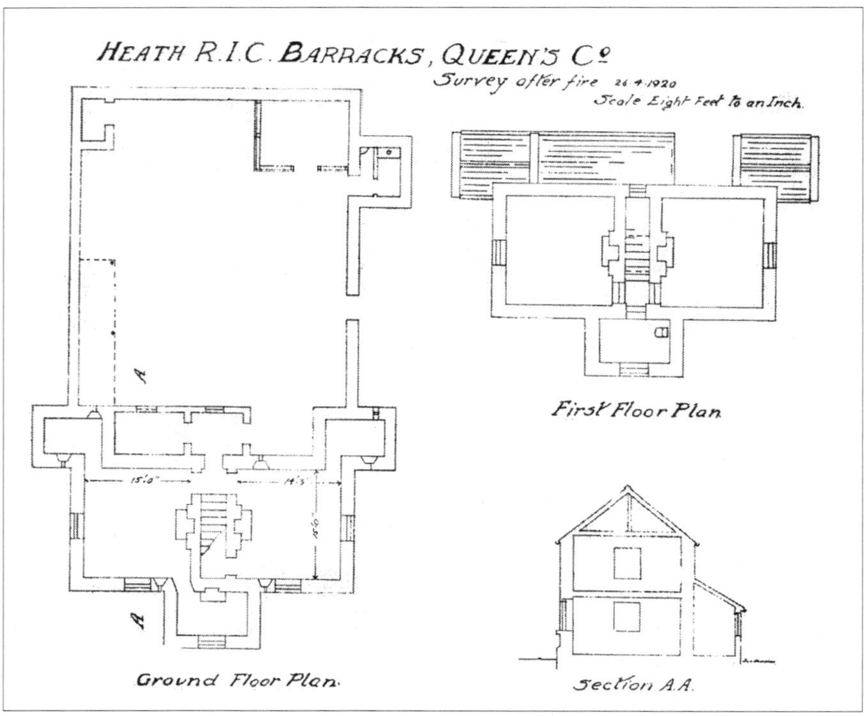

Plans of the former RIC barracks on the Heath, 1920. (*Courtesy of OPW.*)

Irish Prison Service College, Dublin Road

Immediately to the east of the Midlands Prison is the training college for all prison staff in the country, ranging from warders to support staff. Staff quarters had been built in 1982 to replace the demolished cottages alongside the Dublin Road, but in 1984 they were converted into the training college, which was then extended in 2018. The college is now called Brian Stack House.

Garda Síochaná, Abbeyleix Road

This was originally the army barracks, built in 1808 to replace the old cavalry barracks on the north side of the former fort (opposite CBS). The iconic limestone archway dates from 1832, and once had a Russian cannon gun outside the north of the archway. The entire north wing of the barracks was the officers' quarters and mess, the central block was for soldiers, and the south wing was partly a hospital and partly sergeants' quarters.

After the British Army moved out following Irish independence in 1922, the Irish Army occupied the barracks until 1932, after which it was adapted for Garda Síochaná use. In recent decades, the original drill ground (for marching practice) on the north side of the barracks was developed as government offices.

The 1911 Census recorded the Leinster Regiment in the barracks, with forty-five soldiers, all Irish and Catholic, except for four Englishmen (three Anglican, and one Catholic).

Besides an army garrison in Portlaoise, the town also had a constabulary barracks for everyday police work which was stationed in different houses over the generations. The Irish Constabulary was established in 1822 and changed its name to the Royal Irish Constabulary in 1867. The RIC were armed, unlike the Dublin Metropolitan Police, who were unarmed.

For the 1901 Census, the RIC barracks was at 1 Market Square, comprising a head constable, two sergeants, and six constables, all Catholics except for one 'Established Church' (Anglican).

The RIC barracks was at 13 Market Square (south-east corner beside Main Street) for the 1911 Census, comprising head constable, sergeant, two acting sergeants, and six constables, all Catholic, except for two Anglican constables.

Out on the Great Heath of Maryborough, there was a small two-storey RIC barracks, just north of the present golf clubhouse. It was very isolated, on a slightly elevated site, commanding extensive views of the surrounding flat countryside in the days before any trees were planted by the golf club. The building was surrounded by yards and boundary walls, almost military style, and narrow vertical slots in the ground-floor elevations were seemingly intended as gun loops if the windows had to be shuttered. Small projecting spaces at the north-east and north-west corners of the building were possibly vantage points for defence purposes, and may have doubled as prisoner cells (the north-west one is still standing). The Census for 1911 records a sergeant, his wife, his two children, and one constable in this barracks.

The building was damaged in a fire on 26 April 1920, during the War of Independence, and may have remained derelict thereafter. Surely a very lonely station for the brave inhabitants.

Courthouse, Main Street

The original courthouse on this site dated from at least 1766 but was destroyed by a fire in 1782. The gaol behind it facing Church Street was built in 1789, and its noble appearance suggests that it might have been intended as a courthouse, or maybe the front portion for that purpose.

The present overbearing courthouse on Main Street was built in 1805, enlarged in 1876, and an ugly extension added to the west side in 1911 (thankfully, the attic storey was recently removed). There are two large courtrooms now, with court offices above.

Prior to the present system of local government, the grand jury performed the same functions, holding their meetings in the grand jury room at first-floor level in the courthouse. After the new system was introduced in 1899, the county council was also based in the courthouse, with the library located in the empty former gaol behind, until County Hall was built in 1982 on JFL Avenue.

SIX

Miscellaneous

Cinemas

The Electric Cinema, at the Bridge Street end of Well Road (formerly New Road), was opened in November 1914 by the Delaney family, rebuilt in 1928, and finally closed in 1969. The building is still standing and is now a restaurant. The town gas generator produced electricity for the lighting and projectors, long before electricity was adopted in the town by the shops and other businesses.

The Coliseum Cinema was built in 1935, about halfway down Bull Lane on the west side. Its stage was also used for musicals and variety shows. The cinema was rebuilt with two screens after a fire in 1985, and it closed in 2000.

Nowadays, cinema buffs enjoy the facilities of the five-screen ODEON cinema on Church Street.

Dunamaise Arts Centre, Church Street

The former gaol behind the courthouse was used as the public library and council offices from the 1920s until the new County Hall opened in 1982 on JFL Avenue. The gaol was redeveloped in the 1990s, including infilling the central yard, and was finally opened as the Dunamaise Arts Centre in 1999, retaining the impressive front wall and perimeter timber roof trusses from the gaol. The centre now houses a theatre (which is used once a week for films), exhibition space, art classes, and café.

Macra na Feirme

This young farmers' club, which is a nationwide social organisation, opened in 1955 on Well Road on the site of the old gasworks. The site was donated by Mr V.G. Hinds, and the original main dancing hall was 30ft by 52ft. The building has been extended and is still in use.

Danceland, Well Road

The Coliseum Ballroom (not to be confused with the Coliseum Cinema on Bull Lane) was located just a short distance to the south of the Electric Cinema, having been founded just after the Second World War. The 1960s was the heyday of the showband era, with the likes of Joe Dolan, Big Tom and Brendan Boyer, and former Taoiseach Albert Reynolds operated a string of dance halls around the midlands. He acquired the Coliseum around 1961 and renamed it Danceland, running it for about ten years until it was demolished by the council to make way for JFL Avenue.

Bannon's Hall, Station Road

This was an intimate dance hall in the 1940s and '50s, where the Toby Bannon Band played. The building is now a furniture shop, Reliable House Furnishers, run by the two Rowan brothers, which started here in 1969. The original maple dancefloor is still there and also the stage at the east end, one foot above the floor. Originally the building was small and narrow, on an east–west axis, with a double-pitched roof, but the Rowans added an extension to make it square shaped and also built a mezzanine floor.

St Joseph's Accordion Band

Portlaoise had a brass and reed band up until 1954, with its origins going back to the British Army presence in the town. A few local men then founded the Portlaoise Accordion Band in 1957, operating initially from Stradbally Road, and since 1985 from a purpose-built hall in Factory Lane, off Grattan Street. The band, using button accordions, performs at all major public events, including the annual St Patrick's Day Parade, and big football and hurling matches in O'Moore Park stadium. The band also travels to perform in other towns, and even overseas.

Portlaoise also has CBS and Presentation accordion bands, which perform at various public events.

The Heath Golf Club

The 1839 Ordnance Survey map shows the Great Heath of Maryborough, with a roughly oblong-shaped racecourse to the north of Heath House, and the Stand House (in ruins) just outside the south side of the track. To the north of the Stand House was a constabulary barracks. There was a national school and the ruins of a Catholic chapel to the west of the course, and a Catholic chapel and graveyard to the east of the course. The old school is now derelict, since there is a new school nearby, and the chapel foundations are still visible.

The Queen's County Heath Golf Club was founded in 1889, and rebuilt and renovated the old Stand House as their clubhouse. An early twentieth-century Ordnance Survey map shows 'Stand House' with attached dispensary, but no golf course. The golf club was reconstituted as the Heath Golf Club in 1930, again using the Stand House as their clubhouse, and it was increased to eighteen holes in 1971. In 1991, a fine new clubhouse was built slightly to the south of the old clubhouse, and the latter was then demolished. The club machine shed now stands on the site of the former constabulary barracks, and thankfully a portion of the barracks' limestone walls is still standing and is well worth preserving. This might seem an unusual place for a police barracks, but in fact the position is elevated, commanding a great view of the surrounding Great Heath of Maryborough.

The Great Heath is a smaller version of the Curragh in County Kildare, and the land is still commonage, with today's sheep farmers grazing their animals on the golf course (which helps to keep the grass trim!). The Rathshane, an ancient raised mound of earth or fortification called a 'ringfort', is still in position towards the north-east end of the course at Hole 13, beside the GAA club.

The army rifle range was once located to the south of Heath Lodge Demesne, with the target area in the woods and a maximum range of 500 yards.

Ordnance Survey map (1889) of the Great Heath of Maryborough, with the racecourse clearly marked. (*Courtesy of Trinity College Dublin.*)

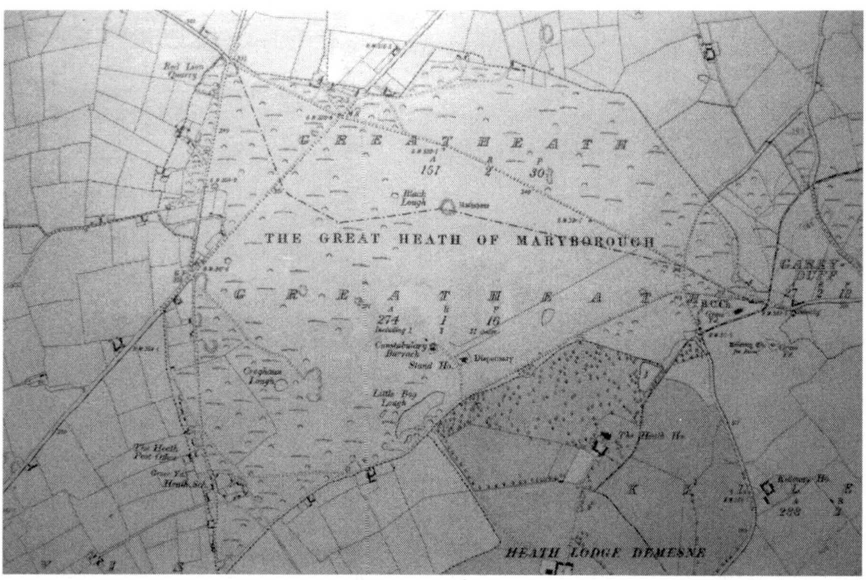

Ordnance Survey map (1907) of the Great Heath of Maryborough, without the racecourse. Note the constabulary barracks, Stand House, and dispensary near the bottom, but no golf course. (*Courtesy of Trinity College Dublin.*)

Portlaoise Golf Club, Abbeyleix Road

This modern club, opposite the O'Moore GAA stadium, was founded in 1995. However, there was a short-lived golf course on this land around one hundred years ago, as shown on the Ordnance Survey map of 1907. This was referred to in sports literature as the Maryborough Golf Club from 1903 to 1916, but it reverted to farmland thereafter. The McEvoy family developed and own the present club; they had farmed the land for generations before recent diversification into golfing.

Leisure Centre, Ridge Road

The original swimming pool opened in 1972 and was replaced by the present modern complex in 2006, comprising pool, gym, meeting rooms, and an all-weather Astroturf football pitch.

Market House/Town Hall, Market Square

The original market house, including a beam scales for weighing products, was built in 1803, and lasted until 1885, when it was replaced by an impressive Town Hall (including weighbridge). There was a serious fire in 1945, and the charming building was demolished in 1949. The Marian Shrine, erected in 1954, now stands on the site.

The grand jury was the local government system in operation up to 1899, and the members met in the grand jury room above the two courts in the courthouse, a tradition that was continued by the county council until their new office block and chamber was built in 1982, on the south side of JFL Avenue. An additional office block was built in 2003, linked to the 1982 building by a long corridor.

The council is a great supporter of the arts, and the foyer contains a 1998 bust of James Fitzmaurice, a short coin-encrusted branch of St Fintan's Tree in a glass case, and a small panel of Mountmellick plain embroidery (white on white) by the Irish Countrywomen's Association (ICA) from 2016. The long corridor link has seven beautiful panels of stained glass, created by Nora Duggan in 2004, depicting various aspects of Laois life. At the front of the building, there is a big bronze statue of James Fintan Lawlor (1807–1849) from Tinakill House, Raheen, the work of Rory Breslin of Mayo in 2007.

A very large market house was built in the square in Mountrath c.1748, and was later bemoaned by many truck drivers on their way to Limerick. After lying idle for decades, it was demolished 1964. The RTÉ Archives has a nice clip from 1962, in which locals gave their opinions on what should become of the derelict building!

War Memorial, Millview Memorial Park, Ridge Road

This ornate masonry monument was erected in 1928 in the centre of the road at Bank Place, at the junction of Church Street and Railway Street, where there was previously a circular fountain/lamp, plus a nearby hand-operated water pump. The monument was taken apart by hand and moved to its present location in 2001, when the council was flush with funds.

Fire Station, Dublin Road

The original station was built in 1958, set back from the road behind the present building, which dates from 2003.

Rock of Dunamase

The Rock is actually a substantial ruined castle built on top of a stone hill in the twelfth century, on the site of a ninth-century fort. Strongbow had it for a while in first half of the thirteenth century. The last resident was Sir John Parnell, grandfather of Charles Stuart Parnell. The views from the summit on a good day are well worth the gentle climb.

Emo Court

This fine classical house was commissioned by John Dawson (of the same family that gave its name to Dawson Street in Dublin), 1st Earl of Portarlington, in 1790, but was not finally finished until 1874. The initial design was by James Gandon, who was responsible for such classical buildings as the Four Courts and Custom House in Dublin, but other architects worked on Emo Court over the following eighty years.

After lying empty during the First World War years, the 11,000-acre estate was bought by the Land Commission in 1920, and they sold the individual farms to the tenant farmers, in return for an indefinite annual small repayment (annuity). Emo Court then lay empty for ten years, until the house and 280 acres (another 32 acres bought in 1938) was sold for £2,000 to the Society of Jesus (Jesuits) Order of teaching priests, for use as a novitiate called St Mary's. A two-storey bachelor wing was built to the west of the house (approached by a long, curved corridor off the main house), containing eight small bedrooms (or 'cells') on each floor. The rotunda and drawing room of the main house were converted into a chapel, with the marble altar directly underneath the dome. The main classroom had a large Evie Hone 'cartoon' (template) for part of her 1952 stained-glass window depicting the Crucifixion, for Eton College Chapel in Windsor, England. In 1958, the central attic conversion was made, comprising a recreation room sized 96ft by 22½ft, set between the existing second-floor wings, and almost hidden from public view. The famous Jesuit Fr Browne, whose real vocation was photography, lived here from 1930 to 1957. The 20-acre Emo Lake provided recreational facilities for the young trainee priests.

Nineteenth-century maps show 'Site of Castle' near the south-west of the house, and a nearby field called 'Jack's Hovel'. The field to the north of the house was called 'The Clucker'.

The priests sold Emo for £40,000 in 1969 to Major Cholmeley-Harrison, who spent a fortune restoring the property, and generously donated it to the State in 1995. The OPW now manages the property, which is open to the public for wonderful walks all year round, and for house tours during the summer months. The first floor of the former bachelors' quarters is now a café.

James Fitzmaurice

James Christopher Fitzmaurice was born in Dublin in 1898, and his family moved to Portlaoise when he was aged 3. His father was a warder in the prison, and the family lived in one of the small prison-owned cottages, listed as 27 Beladd in the 1911 Census. He joined the British Army while underage and was in the Royal Air Force during the latter part of the First World War. Fitzmaurice then came back to Ireland and eventually ended up in the Irish Air Force at Baldonnel, County Dublin.

No one had completed a transatlantic flight from Europe to America (much harder than vice versa, because of the winds), until a freelance German pilot, Hermann Köhl, backed by a wealthy German sponsor, Baron Günther von Hünefeld, made their second attempt on 12 April 1928, flying a German Junkers W 33, called the Bremen D-1167. They chose James Fitzmaurice, then commandant of the newly formed Irish Air Corps at Baldonnel, as the co-pilot and navigator, and the three of them completed the difficult 36½-hour journey from Baldonnel to the tiny island of Greenly in Canada, where a heroes' welcome awaited them.

Fitzmaurice died in Dublin in 1965 and is buried in the small family plot in Glasnevin Cemetery. The family cottage in front of Portlaoise Prison was demolished some years ago.

The county council acquired the large Odlums Mill site on Church Avenue in recent years, and laid out the James Fitzmaurice Plaza (stone paving and lawn), including an abstract piece of metal artwork, in memory of the Dubliner who was part of the German mission to fly across the Atlantic, from east to west, in 1928.

Dr Bartholomew Mosse

Annefield House, on the Dublin Road, just to the north of the Catholic church, was the birthplace in 1712 of Dr Mosse, who founded the fine Rotunda Maternity Hospital in the centre of Dublin in 1757, reputed to be the world's first charitable 'lying-in hospital' for pregnant women. That hospital was designed and built to withstand the test of time, and still features a beautiful 'baby-themed' chapel on the first floor.

The ringfort is depicted in this charming painting by Monica McCormick (1999), one of a series hanging in the Heath Golf Club. (*Courtesy of the Heath Golf Club.*)

Mr Pierce Grace and Mrs M. Bolger, first captains, 1930/31, long before equal rights became law. (*Courtesy of the Heath Golf Club.*)

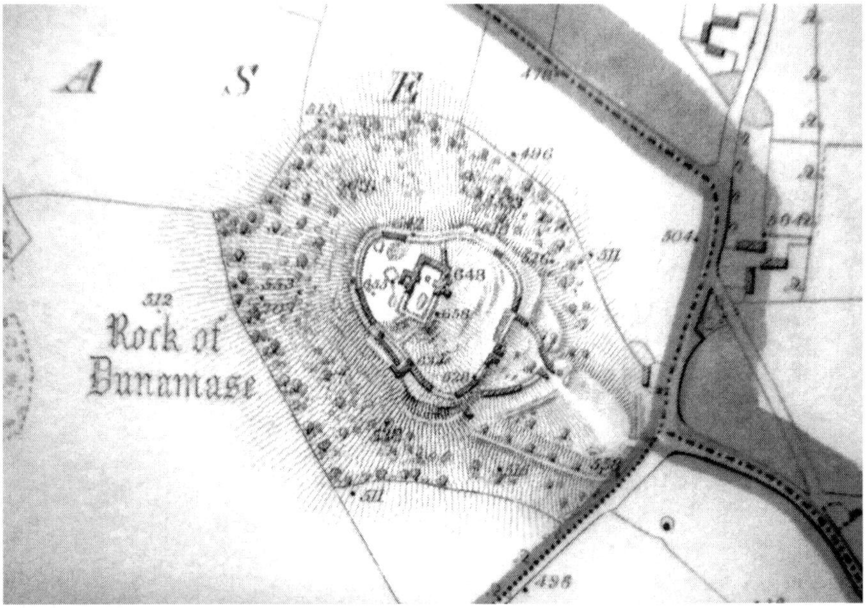

Ordnance Survey map (1839) of the Rock of Dunamase. (*Courtesy of Trinity College Dublin.*)

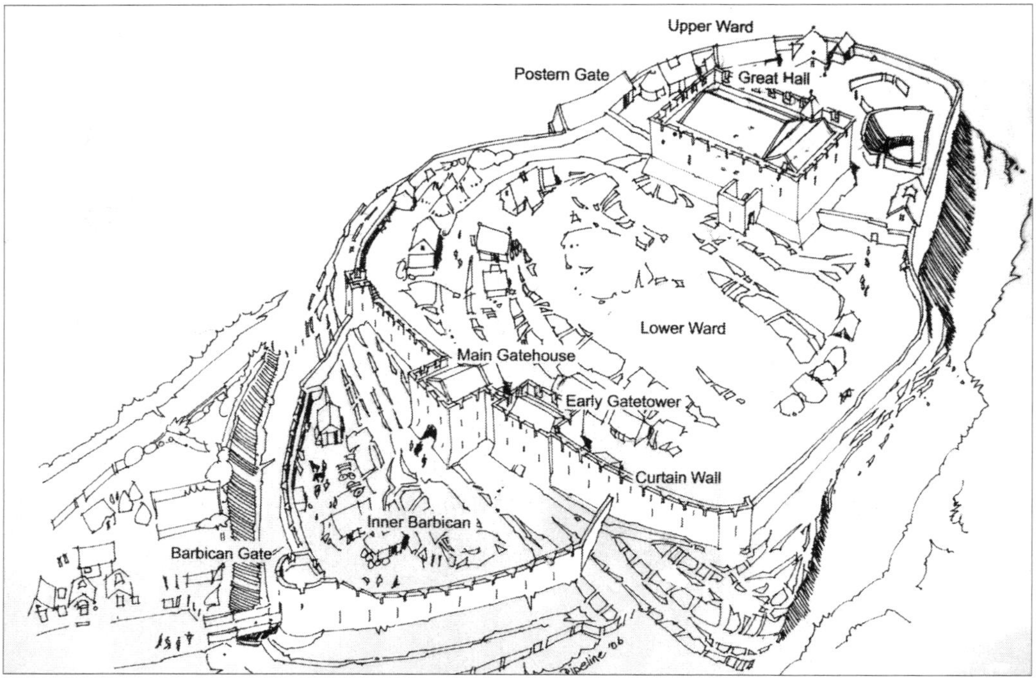

Good schematic diagram of the Rock of Dunamase. (*Courtesy of Office of Public Works.*)

The substantial ruins of the Rock of Dunamase castle are fully accessible.

Looking down from the Rock of Dunamase towards Holy Trinity church.

Emo Court facades are plastered, with stone embellishments. The two-storey bachelor building on the left was built by the Jesuits and is now the café.

The lake-elevation of Emo Court is as attractive as the front. Note the copper-clad dome, which sits above the internal rotunda.

The Jesuits sited their altar under the copper-clad dome of Emo Court. (*Courtesy of Jesuit Archives.*)

Class of Jesuit novices who had just taken their First Vows, pictured in Emo Court in 1961. (*Courtesy of Jesuit Archives.*)

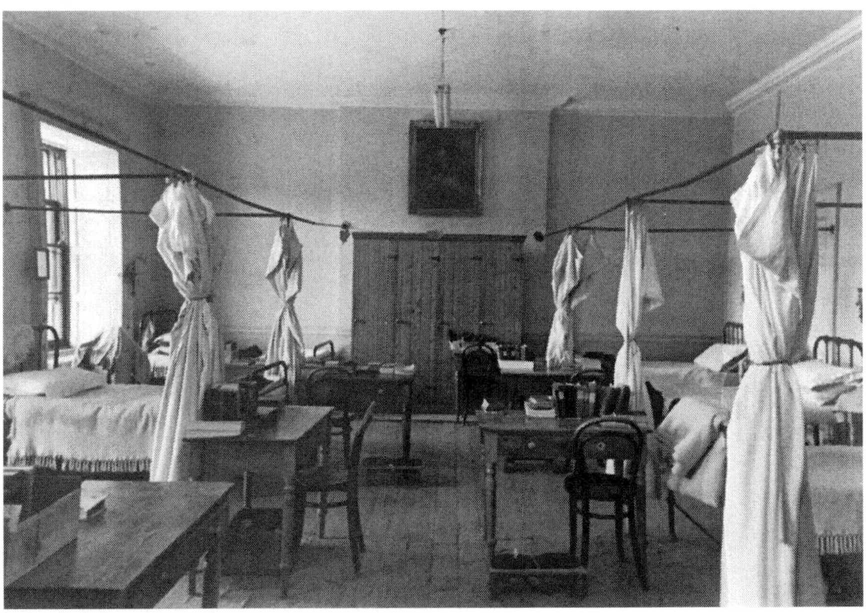

The Jesuit dormitory in the main house of Emo Court was known as the 'Camerata'. (*Courtesy of Jesuit Archives.*)

Fr Donal O'Sullivan teaching Jesuit novices in Emo Court in 1954. Note the Evie Hone crucifixion 'cartoon' on the back wall. (*Courtesy of Jesuit Archives.*)

Postcard of 'French chateau-style' Town Hall in Portlaoise, looking towards the Mountrath Road. (*Courtesy of Laois Local Studies.*)

Above: The 2007 bronze statue of James Fintan Lawlor in front of the council chamber.

Left: The 1954 Marian Shrine stands on the site of the former Town Hall.

Meeting chamber of Laois County Council.

One of the charming stained-glass panels by Nora Duggan in the link corridor of the council offices.

The War Memorial dates from 1928, and was moved to Millview Park in 2001.

This restored '1-horsepower fire engine' hangs over the staircase of the modern fire station opposite the prison.

Portlaoise senior football team, 1958. (*Courtesy of Redmonds Photography, Roscrea.*)

Laois SFC, 1970s. (*Courtesy of Redmonds Photography, Roscrea.*)

Reopening of O'Moore Park in May 1986. (*Courtesy of Laois Local Studies.*)

St Patrick's Day Parade, 1985, with St Joseph's Accordion Band. (*Courtesy of Laois Local Studies.*)

Portlaoise Boxing Club, 1967. (*Courtesy of Laois Local Studies.*)

The 1928 celebration of the *Bremen* flying east to west across the Atlantic. Left to right: Köhl, Fitzmaurice, Hünefeld. (*Courtesy of National Library of Ireland.*)

Above: Mountrath Market House was demolished in 1964. (*Courtesy of Hugh Doran Collection, Irish Architectural Archive.*)

Left: The Coliseum Cinema in Bull Lane was a popular social venue, as seen from this 1948 poster. (*Courtesy of Ryan's Pub, Main Street.*)